EFFORTLESS JAPAN TRAVEL

HOW ANYONE CAN UNLOCK AUTHENTIC EXPERIENCES WITH EXPERT PLANNING, CULTURAL WISDOM, AND A SMART BUDGET

ROBBIN ALLEN

CONTENTS

INTRODUCTION

Picture yourself in the heart of a bustling Tokyo neighborhood, enveloped by towering neon signs, cutting-edge technology, and a bustling crowd that engulfs you. Then, as if by magic, you turn a corner and suddenly discover an oasis of tranquility—an idyllic garden where graceful koi fish glide through a serene pond, meticulously groomed trees provide shade, and the distant murmur of a waterfall soothes your senses.

It's a stark and captivating contrast, a moment that epitomizes Japan's magnetic duality. But the question arises: how do you uncover these hidden treasures amidst the hustle and bustle? That's precisely where this guide steps in, extending a hand to offer you exclusive insights, cultural revelations, and practical guidance, empowering you to navigate Japan with the flair of a seasoned local.

Japan beckons travelers with an endless array of compelling reasons to visit. Whether your heart longs for an immersive exploration of Japan's rich history and culture through its numerous UNESCO World Heritage Sites, the exhilarating thrill of a high-speed ride aboard the lightning-fast Shinkansen trains, or a culinary journey through the diverse flavors of Japanese cuisine, a Japanese escapade guarantees discovery and excitement at every twist and turn.

The country is dominated by expansive woodlands and towering mountains, offering ample opportunities for nature enthusiasts. While iconic Mount Fuji is an undeniable highlight, don't overlook the chance to explore less-frequented natural wonders like the enchanting Arashiyama bamboo forest or the serene Ritsurin landscape gardens on Shikoku Island. Additionally, Japan stands as a premier global destination for witnessing the splendid springtime spectacle of cherry blossoms blooming.

If you can't visit during the spring, summer also has something in store for you, with the colorful Matsuri festivals taking place nationwide. These traditional festivities honor legendary historical occurrences and various deities associated with specific shrines in the towns where they are held. A multitude of Matsuri festivals showcase grand processions featuring colossal floats, vibrant parades, and dazzling displays of fireworks.

During the winter months, you can immerse yourself in the mesmerizing winter illuminations that adorn the city streets throughout the holiday season. For those who revel in winter sports, seizing the opportunity to snowboard and ski in Japan at its numerous resorts is an absolute must, given that Japanese powder snow is globally renowned as some of the finest. As such, the country boasts a wealth of top-tier ski destinations. The Sapporo Snow Festival in Hokkaido is also a popular choice. Here, you'll be treated to a captivating array of astonishing ice sculptures, some inspired by beloved pop culture icons and characters.

If your love for Japan was kindled by manga and anime, Tokyo is your dream destination, offering an array of immersive anime-themed attractions. Dive into the world of manga characters at Akihabara and Ikebukuro, or further satisfy your anime cravings with a visit to the colossal Pokémon Mega Center Tokyo, where exclusive Japanese Pokémon merchandise awaits you. It's an anime lover's paradise!

While you're in Tokyo, you can also view the Tokyo Skytree, the tallest tower in the capital. Additionally, you can find some excellent examples of traditional Japanese architecture throughout the country, such as the city of Ise, where the majestic Ise shrines are located.

What's more, the Japanese are renowned across the globe for their exceptional courtesy, warmth, and hospitality.

You'll find that in Japan, people often go out of their way to assist you whenever you seek their help or guidance. They also take immense pride in maintaining cleanliness. When you first set foot in the country, you might be pleasantly surprised by the immaculate streets. Hotels and restaurants, in particular, are meticulously clean, exuding delightful aromas, and subject to regular and thorough cleaning routines.

Japan also consistently ranks as one of the world's safest nations, boasting one of the lowest global crime rates. It's common to find doors left unlocked by Japanese residents, witness children confidently navigating the subway alone, and enjoy nighttime strolls in the cities without safety concerns.

With all these captivating reasons to visit, you'd imagine that most people would jump at the chance to book their trips. However, many are held back by a few common concerns. One of the first things you might be pondering is the language barrier, especially once you venture beyond the major cities. English isn't widely spoken, which can make everyday interactions, reading signs, and even ordering food feel like quite the challenge. This can sometimes make fully immersing yourself in Japan's vibrant culture seem a bit daunting.

Additionally, the mere thought of cultural misunderstandings is enough to invoke anxiety. Japan boasts a wonderfully rich and unique culture with its own customs and social norms. It's easy to accidentally step on cultural toes without even realizing it, which could lead to some awkward moments and misunderstandings during your travels.

Budgeting is another thing that might be on your mind. Japan is known for its relatively high cost of living, and it's common for travelers to find themselves a bit surprised by how quickly expenses can add up. This can be a tricky thing to navigate and might mean missing out on some incredible experiences.

While you may be drawn to Japan for its distinct culture and history, finding genuine encounters and avoiding tourist traps may feel like an impossible feat. Then there's the intricate web of Japan's transportation system, especially the extensive train network. It's fantastic in terms of efficiency, but planning routes, especially between cities or when exploring off-the-beaten-path can be incredibly puzzling.

I wholeheartedly understand the challenges travelers face when planning their trips. I vividly recall the linguistic hurdles, budgetary tightropes, and cultural misunderstandings that often clouded my own journeys in Japan. Understanding Japan's rich customs and history required years of exploration, and navigating their intricate methods of travel almost had me go for the much more expensive and traffic-ridden option of renting a car! Yet, it is precisely these challenges that have fueled my determination to sit down and write this book.

I'm here to assist you in overcoming all the hurdles I, and many others, have faced. I'll ensure your journey to Japan doesn't just go smoothly but is also deeply enriching, allowing you to savor the culture, history, and beauty of this incredible country. Within the pages of this book, you will gain numerous shortcuts, like:

- **efficient travel planning:** Gain invaluable assistance in streamlining your travel preparations. From securing flights and accommodations to crafting an itinerary that optimizes your time and enriches your experiences, this guide is your trusted travel companion for efficient planning.
- **cultural immersion:** Unveil the profound cultural insights this guide unveils, offering you a deeper understanding of Japanese customs and traditions. It's your key to immersing yourself fully in Japan's rich culture.
- **smart budgeting:** Discover practical advice for budgeting your Japanese journey, complete with cost estimates and savvy tips for saving on accommodations, dining, and transportation.
- **language assistance:** Navigate the language barrier easily, thanks to the essential Japanese phrases and language tips provided in this guide.

Communicate effortlessly with locals and traverse Japan confidently.

- **customized experiences:** Whether your heart yearns for historical wonders, culinary delights, natural wonders, or the pulse of vibrant city life, this guide provides recommendations and itineraries to suit your unique travel preferences.
- **stress reduction:** Leave travel-related stress behind as you tap into expert advice and resources, knowing you have a reliable companion for planning and decision-making.
- **authentic encounters:** Forge genuine connections with Japan and its people. This guide opens doors to authentic cultural experiences and meaningful interactions with locals.
- **enhanced appreciation:** Immerse yourself in the beauty, history, and significance of Japan's sites armed with cultural wisdom and historical context provided in this guide, deepening your appreciation.
- **gracefully throughout Japan:** Empower yourself with knowledge and insights from this guide, bolstering your confidence to explore Japan on your terms. Craft enduring memories and relish an enriching travel experience, knowing you're well-prepared.

After reading this book, you'll emerge well-prepared to plan and enjoy a fulfilling and immersive journey through

Japan. Armed with newfound knowledge, you'll glide through the potential hurdles and travel gracefully throughout Japan. This guide will empower you to dive headfirst into the nation's distinctive culture, creating unforgettable memories along the way. You'll exude confidence in your financial planning, seamless communication, and the ability to unearth genuine encounters. Additionally, your trip will be marked by a profound appreciation for Japan's resplendent history, culture, and age-old customs.

View this travel guide as your trusted companion. By utilizing the knowledge within these pages, you'll be able to immerse yourself in Japan's culture fully. This guide will make you feel like you're having a conversation with a dear friend who's been there and done that. It'll empower you to overcome challenges, navigate seamlessly, and embrace Japan with open arms. So, what are you waiting for? The Land of the Rising Sun awaits!

1

PLANNING YOUR TRIP

The magic of a trip to Japan starts long before you set foot on Japanese soil. It begins with the joy of meticulous planning, the exhilaration of eager anticipation, and the promise of unforgettable experiences.

ESTABLISH YOUR TRAVEL PURPOSE AND OBJECTIVES

While traveling is wonderful on its own, infusing it with specific goals can elevate your experience to a whole new level of significance. When you envision your dream destinations and experiences, it can lead to a profound exploration of self-discovery, personal development, and unforgettable moments.

Setting travel goals doesn't just imbue your adventures with purpose; it also guides you during your trip planning. This is important since Japan is a place brimming with incredible places to explore, which can cause you to feel overwhelmed. Yet, by setting clear objectives, you not only streamline your choices but also maintain unwavering motivation throughout the entire process. Let's go over a few examples of goals you can set to ensure your trip to Japan is as purposeful as it is thrilling.

- **Walk the Kumano Kodo:** Experience a one-of-a-kind blend of history, culture, and spirituality on the Kumano Kodo routes that weave through Japan's serene landscapes.
- **Explore Japan's UNESCO world heritage sites:** Journey to iconic landmarks like Kyoto's temples, Hiroshima's Peace Memorial, or Nikko's shrines.
- **Embark on a scenic Japanese train adventure:** Take unforgettable rail journeys in Japan, such as the scenic Sagano Scenic Railway or the Seven Stars in Kyushu.
- **Witness wildlife in natural Japanese habitats:** Encounter awe-inspiring wildlife like snow monkeys in Nagano or sea turtles in Okinawa—these encounters with Japan's majestic creatures will leave lasting impressions.
- **Dine at Michelin-starred Japanese restaurants:** Since Japan boasts a whopping 414 Michelin-starred restaurants, it's only fitting to visit at least one of them and savor their delicious food.

- **Conquer famous Japanese mountains:** Challenge yourself by climbing iconic Japanese mountains like Mount Fuji or trekking to remote spots like the Japan Alps for unforgettable views and personal accomplishments.
- **Discover traditional Japanese crafts:** Immerse yourself in Japan's rich artistic heritage by learning traditional crafts like pottery, calligraphy, or tea ceremony. This hands-on experience will deepen your connection with Japan's culture and allow you to create beautiful keepsakes.
- **Ride the waves:** Learn the art of surfing in captivating Japanese destinations, whether it's the beaches of Chiba, Okinawa, or other coastal gems.

THINGS TO CONSIDER WHEN PLANNING YOUR TRIP

Choosing when to travel to Japan is influenced by a myriad of factors. From affordability to climate and seasonal appeal, various elements come into play. In the following section, I'll walk you through some decision-making factors and offer valuable tips to simplify the task of planning your trip.

Where Do You Want to Go?

To help refine your choices of the places you want to explore in Japan, consider crafting a travel bucket list focused on specific regions or cities within Japan that truly captivate your imagination. Are you drawn to hidden gems rather than well-trodden paths? While many might prefer the former, it's important to acknowledge that the world's most-visited attractions hold their popularity for good reason – they are truly incredible experiences!

Similarly, If the idea of experiencing the tranquility of Kyoto's temples appeals to you more than wandering through Tokyo's bustling neighborhoods, it can simplify your decision-making process. It's all about preference.

The Season and Weather

When it comes to planning your visit to Japan, factoring in the season is crucial. Opting for travel during the peak tourist season or the off-season can significantly impact your experience. If flexibility permits, targeting months with favorable weather during the shoulder season can be ideal, offering a balance between affordability and fewer crowds.

Now, as for your personal weather preferences, do you lean towards the warmth of summer or the chill of winter? While traveling during the off-season can yield savings and advantages, it's essential to assess whether the weather conditions align with your planned activities. After all, you wouldn't want to find yourself unable to enjoy outdoor excursions due to heavy rainfall during the rainy season in Japan. Additionally, if you're planning a ski trip in Japan, booking during the early shoulder season may not be wise if it's been an unusually mild winter.

If time constraints limit your flexibility, you might have to adapt to the prevailing weather conditions. Therefore, thorough research, weather checks, and careful consideration of the seasons should guide your travel plans in Japan.

The Cost of Living

Japan is known for its high cost of living, and Tokyo consistently ranks among the top ten most expensive cities globally. However, there are various other places where the cost of living is more reasonable, including popular cities like Hiroshima, Fukuoka, and Sapporo. Additionally, charming tropical destinations like Yakushima and Amami Oshima provide more budget-friendly alternatives. Notably, Kumamoto and Okayama offer more affordable rental choices compared to other major urban areas in Japan. Similarly, locations like Sendai and Oita generally have lower living expenses, especially when it comes to utilities, groceries, and dining out, in comparison to the country's largest cities.

Therefore, before your visit, conduct thorough research on the cost of living in your chosen destination. Utilize collaborative online databases like Numbeo to compile a comprehensive list of typical expenses, including dining at local restaurants, enjoying a cup of coffee, utilizing public transportation, and more. Additionally, services like Expatistan enable you to make side-by-side comparisons between the cost of living in your current city and that of your intended destination in Japan, ensuring you make informed decisions about your travel budget.

Creating a Travel Budget

Budget considerations often play a pivotal role when it comes to selecting your travel destination in Japan. You don't need a fortune to embark on a memorable journey, but striking the right balance between comfort and expenses is essential. So, here are a few key factors to consider while determining your budget:

- Does your country have favorable currency exchange rates with the yen?
- Can you leverage airline or hotel miles and points to offset some costs?
- Are you open to flying with a budget carrier, or do you prefer the indulgence of business or first class?
- Does your chosen destination necessitate the purchase of specific travel accessories?
- Are you more inclined to book a room in a traditional hotel or opt for the communal atmosphere of a hostel?

- Do you lean towards boutique hotels, or is the idea of staying in an Airbnb more appealing?
- Are you inclined towards luxurious getaways or aiming to keep your expenses in check?

Understanding the expenses associated with airfare, accommodations, and visa requirements for your chosen destination will help you gauge which options align with your financial comfort zone. In the next chapter, we'll delve into strategies to make the most of your budget while savoring the wonders of Japan.

Spontaneity Versus Planning

Planning a trip is undoubtedly valuable, but even with a well-structured itinerary, you might be inclined to make changes or trade your original plan for new experiences. Personally, I've discovered that meticulous planning is a handy skill, yet some of the most unforgettable moments occur when you embrace spontaneity.

It's perfectly okay to alter your plans while on the road. I've met many fellow travelers who thrive on last-minute decisions, factoring in flight prices and their eagerness to explore. While this approach may not suit everyone and can sometimes deprive organized individuals of the joys of thorough planning, it offers a different kind of thrill.

Chart your journey the way you envision it, knowing you can adjust it when you arrive at your destination. Along the way, you'll encounter places where you'll want to linger and others that may be less enticing. Some locales may prove pricier than anticipated, while others could pleasantly surprise you with their affordability. Weather can also throw surprises your way, impacting flights and creating an element of uncertainty. Thus, striking a harmonious balance between well-thought-out plans and spur-of-the-moment decisions is well worth the effort.

Extended Versus Short-Term Travel

The choice of your travel destination should be influenced by your interests and the available time you have. If you only have a week or two to dedicate to your trip, it's wise to focus on a single city or region. The frantic rush to cover as much ground as possible is best avoided. Opting for a single destination during shorter journeys can relieve unnecessary stress and offer a much better experience. On the other hand, going on a long-term vacation, spanning a couple of months or more, opens up a broader range of possibilities.

Your Travel Objectives

Travel burnout can creep up on you, often marked by emotional exhaustion and a sense of detachment or cynicism, especially during long-term travel in new and unfamiliar surroundings. This fatigue can stem from the repetitiveness of your experiences, the constant adaptation to different cultures, and the endless cycle of meeting new people.

If you're seeking a more relaxed vacation, you can narrow down your options. For instance, you might avoid bustling metropolises like Tokyo and opt for serene coastal areas or lakeside retreats. Conversely, if you're in search of an outdoor hiking adventure, rural regions may be more enticing. But why choose when many destinations offer a delightful blend of activities and well-developed tourist infrastructure in the same city or region? With your travel objectives in mind, selecting a destination that captivates all your senses becomes a more straightforward task.

Your Travel Companions

Are you traveling alone, bringing family along, exploring as a couple, or sharing the experience with friends? It goes without saying that the composition of your travel group will significantly influence your choice of destination and activities. The goal is to ensure that the destination caters to the enjoyment of everyone in your party.

If you're traveling as a family with young kids in tow, it's essential to make the journey not only enjoyable but also educational. This means considering activities like sightseeing, age-appropriate museums, and cultural experiences that can enrich their learning. However, if you're planning a romantic escape with your partner, your destination choice will likely lean in a completely different direction. For solo travelers, the preference might be to stay in hostels, as they provide excellent opportunities to meet and socialize with fellow solo adventurers.

Getting a Visa

To explore Japan, you may need to secure a tourist visa in advance of your arrival, a prerequisite that comes with a few exceptions. Notably, Japan extends visa exemption to citizens of several nations, including numerous European countries, the United States, Australia, and Argentina. These countries enjoy the status of visa-exempt nations for tourism purposes, permitting their citizens to stay in Japan for a maximum period of 90 days sans the need for a visa, with Temporary Visitor status automatically bestowed upon them.

If you do need to get a visa, the Japan tourist visa typically allows for a single-entry stay of up to 90 days. Furthermore, tourists have the option to apply for a double-entry visa, which grants the flexibility of going on two short trips to Japan within a six-month timeframe.

SELECTING A TRAVEL SEASON: PROS AND CONS OF DIFFERENT TIMES OF THE YEAR

Spring

Spring in Japan typically spans from March to May, a season that heralds the arrival of one of the country's most iconic natural phenomena – the cherry blossoms, known as "sakura." Japan's geographical expanse, stretching from north to south, means that sakura make their debut in the southern regions as early as late March before gradually advancing northward. Hokkaido, situated in the northernmost part of Japan, experiences the full splendor of cherry blossoms in May. Spring graces the land with mild weather, making it an ideal season for a diverse array of leisure activities.

While the enchantment of cherry blossom season can't be denied, the question remains: is it truly worth the potential challenges? Besides the unpredictable blooming pattern, which varies from year to year, and the whims of the wind and rain that can scatter the blossoms prematurely, cherry blossoms have become incredibly renowned. Japan has seen a surge in tourists, making the peak cherry blossom season from mid-March to mid-April incredibly crowded. This translates to larger crowds, reduced accommodation availability, increased prices, and the need for extensive preplanning.

Summer

Summer typically spans from June to August in Japan. Given the country's coastal geography, there are numerous places to swim. While you can take a dip in the sea near Tokyo, the remote islands of Okinawa are highly recommended for a more relaxed coastal experience. After the rainy season known as "tsuyu," which lingers from June to late July, concludes, the temperature escalates swiftly. This marks the onset of summer festivals and fireworks taking place across Japan. You can delight in observing these festivals or even join in the spirited dancing at some of them.

Aside from the typical summer crowds, exacerbated by summer vacations occurring worldwide, one of the potential drawbacks of a summer visit to Japan is the sweltering heat and high humidity. Temperatures during this season can range from around 70 to 90 °F (21 to 32 °C), which can become uncomfortable for those unaccustomed to such conditions. Trying to squeeze too many activities into your itinerary can be exhausting in this weather. Whether or not it's worth it largely hinges on your personal tolerance for and enjoyment of this type of climate.

Fall

From September to November, Japan experiences its enchanting fall season. The lingering summer heat begins to dissipate, giving way to the most pleasant and agreeable weather of the year. The pinnacle of this season is the breathtaking transformation of foliage, with leaves changing colors in full splendor from October through late November. Starting in Hokkaido, mountain landscapes gradually shift their hues, painting the country with a vibrant palette of reds, oranges, and yellows. Throughout Japan, destinations renowned for their autumn foliage offer captivating experiences for visitors.

Fall also sets the stage for outdoor sports and leisure activities, making it an ideal time to explore the great outdoors. Additionally, this season brings a culinary delight with its array of seasonal foods, rich in both flavor and nutrition.

Much like spring, fall boasts both allure and potential drawbacks. Embracing the beauty of Kyoto, or fall foliage, entails navigating through increased tourist numbers, reduced accommodation options, elevated accommodation costs, and a necessity for advanced planning, mirroring the challenges of hanami season travel.

Winter

Winter in Japan spans from December to February and ushers in the chilliest season of the year, making it an ideal time to indulge in the therapeutic hot springs scattered across the country. Furthermore, Japan dazzles with a variety of illumination events as the year-end approaches, creating enchanting displays of light. Don't forget to witness the captivating drift ice and the snow-covered vistas that define this magical season. For those seeking leisurely activities, winter offers opportunities for skiing and dog sledding, adding excitement to the chilly months.

The period surrounding New Year's Day in Japan tends to get quite bustling. Tourists from abroad and Japanese locals make the days before, during, and after New Year's Day vibrant and lively. While some find this atmosphere enchanting, filled with the holiday spirit in Japanese style, others seeking tranquility might not find the bustling crowds as enjoyable.

Moreover, since Japanese people enjoy an extended New Year's holiday, accommodations across the country tend to have high occupancy rates, resulting in limited availability and higher prices. Luxury ryokans, in particular, are often booked up nearly a year in advance by returning guests.

During the New Year period in Japan, it's essential to note that starting from late December (typically after Christmas) until several days into January (usually around January 3rd or 4th or even later), many establishments close temporarily, including certain shops, museums, restaurants, and more. While exceptions are increasing, traditionally, one could expect most restaurants to be closed except for high-end dining venues and those situated in department stores and hotels that mainly cater to travelers. Additionally, most temples and shrines remain open around the New Year's holiday.

EXPLORE SEASONAL EVENTS, FESTIVALS, AND ATTRACTIONS

Sapporo Snow Festival

Kicking off the festival calendar in February, this delightful event unfolds in Hokkaido's regional capital, within the picturesque setting of Odori Park. Here, expansive snow and ice sculptures take center stage, attracting visitors worldwide to revel in their icy grandeur.

Hanami and Cherry Blossom Festivals

A tradition observed throughout Japan, Hanami, which translates to "flower viewing," involves picnicking beneath the stunning blooming trees in public parks during this exceptional season. Typically lasting for approximately two weeks in March, the schedule for cherry blossom viewing varies slightly each year.

Takayama Matsuri

The Takayama Matsuri is an annual celebration held in April at Hie Jinja Shrine, affectionately referred to as Sanno-sama. This shrine serves as the protector deity of the southern part of the historic Takayama castle town. Commonly known as the Sanno Festival, it marks the arrival of spring in Takayama, a picturesque city nestled in snow-covered mountains. As the locals revel in the season's warmth, the festival also symbolizes their prayers to the deities for year-round peace and a fruitful harvest. Notable aspects of the festival include the yatai, which are festival floats, and the traditional Karakuri performances.

Sanja Matsuri

Located in the district of Asakusa, Tokyo's foremost festival has called the renowned Sensoji Shrine its home for over two centuries. During this lively celebration, portable shrines housing deities are enthusiastically carried by men sporting traditional loin-cloths alongside local women and children, all united in the vibrant procession. The spectacle, drawing in more than two million spectators each May, is a tradition aimed at securing good fortune and prosperity for the district.

Kyoto Gion Matsuri

The Gion Matsuri is one of Japan's most cherished festivals, gracing the ancient geisha district of Gion each July. Centered around Yasaka Shrine, this spectacular event is a delightful fusion of ornate floats, classical melodies, rhythmic drumming, captivating dance exhibitions, and sacred rituals that span most of the month.

Nachi Fire Festival

Every mid-July, Shingu bursts into life with its annual fire rituals. The festivities commence with solemn Shinto tributes, followed by the adornment and transport of 12 portable shrines to a shrine nestled near a waterfall. The ceremony culminates with a cleansing fire bath believed to purify the shrines.

O-Bon (Festival of the Dead)

Typically occurring in August, this festival is celebrated across Japan. Rooted in Buddhist tradition, it signifies the day when the departed souls visit their earthly relatives. Homes are adorned with lanterns, and offerings are tendered to honor these spirits. As night falls, lanterns are gently set afloat on rivers, serving as beacons to guide the departed souls back to their final resting places.

Nagasaki Kunchi Festival

Nagasaki Kunchi is an autumn festival that takes place in October at Nagasaki's Suwa Shrine, paying homage to the town's guardian deity. The name "Kunchi" draws its inspiration from a Chinese tradition that celebrates the ninth day of the ninth month in the lunar calendar. In Japanese, this day is referred to as "ku-nichi," resembling "Kunchi." The festival's origins can be traced back to 1634, when two courtesans dedicated a song to the shrine. Presently, Nagasaki boasts 58 dance troupes that take turns performing every seven years. Noteworthy performances include the dragon dance and "kokkodesho," a spectacle where forty strong men lift and catch a one-ton "Taikoyama."

CREATING A TIMELINE AND ITINERARY

A travel itinerary serves as a structured plan detailing the destinations you intend to explore during your visit to Japan. It proves invaluable for planning and budgeting for your activities while traveling. Having one readily available simplifies the process of booking flights and accommodation, ensuring all essential information is conveniently compiled into a single place.

Determine the Duration of the Trip

When you begin to craft your itinerary, the first task is to determine your departure date and the intended duration of your trip. A comprehensive travel plan should encompass vital details such as trip dates and destinations, a daily schedule of planned activities, emergency contact particulars, and departure times from transportation hubs.

Create a Realistic, Flexible Itinerary

After you've determined all the important dates and information, it's time to decide on key destinations you want to see and activities you want to partake in. Keep in mind that Japan is filled to the brim with beautiful locations and things to do, so be realistic when planning how you'll be spending the days of your trip.

If your visit is only a week long, it's better to focus your time on one city or region rather than trying to squeeze in as many activities as possible and spending most of your time on trains to different regions. On the other hand, if you're visiting for a month or longer, then you can think about traveling across the country and spending a few days in several cities or regions. Regardless of the length of your trip, remember to schedule rest days to avoid travel burnout.

Allocate Time for Spontaneous Experiences

While your itinerary should serve as a roadmap for your plans, don't be afraid of spontaneity. After all, it's a vacation, and the primary goal is to savor every moment. By conducting thorough research and compiling ideas in advance, you provide room for flexibility. This way, you won't find yourself scrambling to locate good dining options or interesting attractions and activities at the last minute.

Once you arrive at your destination, you'll have the chance to interact with the locals and uncover hidden gems and activities not easily discovered online. Be sure to incorporate these newfound experiences into your itinerary, not only for your own benefit but also to share these valuable insights with friends who may visit Japan in the future.

IN SUMMARY

In this first chapter about planning your trip to Japan, we covered the following topics:

- establishing your travel purpose and objectives
- things to consider when planning your trip
- selecting a travel season
- exploring seasonal events, festivals, and attractions

- creating a timeline and itinerary

As we conclude this chapter, I encourage you to implement these valuable insights. In the upcoming chapter, we'll dive into a pivotal aspect of travel planning: budgeting. We'll help you create a realistic and smart budget that ensures you can make the most of your time in Japan without breaking the bank. So, stay tuned for essential tips and strategies to maximize your travel experience while managing your finances wisely. Your adventure through Japan is just beginning!

2

STRETCHING YOUR YEN

Do you dream of exploring Japan without emptying your wallet? Surprisingly, it's entirely possible to enjoy this captivating country on a budget—or even indulge in luxury without breaking the bank.

COST ESTIMATION

Planning your trip to Japan can feel overwhelming, especially when you're conscious of sticking to a budget. Yet, clearly understanding your financial boundaries, anticipated expenses, and strategies to avoid unnecessary spending can transform your trip into a stress-free and enjoyable experience. Let's explore some ways to create a travel budget that not only keeps your finances in check but also ensures your itinerary is packed with excitement.

What to Budget For

Wondering where to start when it comes to budgeting for your trip? If you're not a seasoned traveler, feeling a bit unsure is perfectly normal. The key is to break it down into categories. Picture your entire journey, from the moment you set off to your return home, and consider how your expenses will unfold along the way. As you do this, create a nifty travel budget spreadsheet that neatly arranges your spending into various categories tailored to Japan.

Transportation

This accounts for the costs associated with reaching Japan and navigating within the country. While many make use of Japan's robust public transport (which we'll explore in depth in the following chapter), some may opt for renting a car when, for example, they plan to explore Hokkaido's beautiful landscapes to travel between scenic spots comfortably. Remember to factor in expenses such as fuel, meals during pit stops, and any vehicle preparations you might need. It's also a good idea to leave a bit of flexibility in your budget, as your transportation plans may evolve during your stay.

Lodging, Taxes, and Fees

Accommodation expenses can make up a substantial part of your budget. The advantage here is that you typically know the exact amount in advance, making it easier to budget accurately. For instance, if you're heading to Kyoto, you might want to set aside a specific amount for staying in a traditional ryokan, complete with tatami mats and a serene garden view.

Food and Dining

Your spending in this category can vary widely based on your culinary preferences and travel destination. Whether you're indulging in Japan's many Michelin-starred restaurants or opting for budget-friendly street food, it's important to account for these costs. If you're more inclined to enjoy takeout or deliveries during your travels, make sure to include those additional charges in your budget.

Internet Access

When you're budgeting for your trip, it's important to allocate funds for staying connected to the internet. Internet access is vital for various purposes during your travels, such as sharing your experiences through photos, navigating unfamiliar streets, and keeping in touch with friends and family back home. To ensure you have a smooth online experience in Japan, you'll want to consider the various methods available for internet access while abroad. All of which we'll explore in detail later in this chapter.

Activities

This category covers the exciting aspects of your journey, such as entrance fees to renowned museums, guided tours to historical sites, thrilling excursions, or even a round of golf on Japan's scenic courses. For instance, if you're exploring the ancient city of Nara, allocate funds for visiting cultural landmarks like Todai-ji Temple and its iconic Great Buddha statue.

Souvenirs

Set aside a portion of your budget for those unique keepsakes and mementos you'll want to bring back from your Japanese escapade. These special items capture the essence of your journey and wouldn't typically find a place in your regular shopping list back home. Whether it's traditional ceramics from Kyoto or handmade crafts from the artisans of Kanazawa, there are plenty of treasures to discover.

Calculating Your Budget

You can budget an estimated daily expenditure of around ¥18,967 ($134) for your trip (excluding internet fees). Typically, you can allocate approximately ¥4,590 ($32) for your daily meals and ¥2,856 ($20) for local transportation. Furthermore, the average cost of accommodation for a couple in Japan comes to ¥17,711 ($125). As a result, an average one-week trip for two people to Japan totals approximately ¥265,540 ($1,873).

TOP PLACES TO EXCHANGE CURRENCY

Banks

Major banks such as Mizuho, MUFG, and SMBC provide currency exchange services; however, their hours of operation are limited, running from 9 a.m. to 3 p.m. on weekdays. While these options are available, managing your expectations regarding exchange rates is important. For potentially more favorable rates, consider prioritizing ATMs located in nearby convenience stores.

Convenience Store ATMs

The most straightforward option for short-term travelers is often withdrawing yen from an ATM using your local bank account. Many ATMs in convenience stores accept Mastercard, VISA, and JCB bank cards, with 7-Eleven ATMs being particularly user-friendly. To address potential language barriers, most ATMs offer multiple language settings to facilitate your transaction.

It's worth noting that not all ATMs in Japan operate around the clock. For instance, ATMs in post offices, which may be your sole option in remote areas, are only available during regular business hours.

Currency Exchange Shops

Upon clearing immigration and customs, you'll find currency exchange shops conveniently available at most Japanese airports, often situated on both sides of the exit, such as at Narita International Airport. In addition to major airports, these facilities are commonly found at significant train stations and select shopping centers throughout the city. Notably, World Currency Shop, which operates under Bank of Tokyo-Mitsubishi UFJ, Travelex, and Daikokuya, boasts numerous branches in Tokyo, simplifying the currency exchange process. However, it's essential to be aware that these establishments may charge substantial commissions.

Now that we've explored everything you need to budget for and options of where you can exchange currency in Japan, it's time to shift our focus to some valuable tips for budget travelers. These insights will help you maximize your finances during your Japanese adventure, ensuring a memorable and cost-effective journey.

TIPS FOR BUDGET TRAVELERS

Booking the Best Flights

Opt for Weekday Flights

Choosing to fly on weekdays, especially Tuesdays and Wednesdays, can save you a lot of money. Flight prices tend to be lower during the workweek, primarily because these days are less popular for travel.

Book Early

Don't assume that last-minute deals are always the cheapest option for securing affordable flight tickets because, more often than not, they aren't. While it's true that flight costs may experience fluctuations, dropping and then potentially rising again in the last few days before departure, this isn't guaranteed. Therefore, the smart approach is to book well in advance, sometimes even up to a year ahead, if the option is available for your desired flight.

Flight tickets tend to be more budget-friendly when they are first released, typically about a year before the scheduled flight. So, it's a good idea to start searching online as soon as the flights you need become available. This is especially crucial if you're planning to travel during school holidays or to a destination hosting a major event. In such cases, prices can skyrocket quickly, so booking early is your best defense.

Use Your Credit Card to Book Flights

There are several benefits to using a credit card for your flight booking. One significant advantage is the added protection you receive when making larger purchases. Keep in mind that this protection might not apply to your debit card, so it's essential to verify the terms in advance. Additionally, credit cards are more convenient for spending abroad and typically offer more favorable exchange rates compared to debit cards.

Beware of Hidden Expenses

Remember that seemingly cheap flight tickets with budget airlines can sometimes come with hidden costs. It's important to check for additional expenses such as air taxes, baggage fees, or seat selection charges before making your purchase. Additionally, be cautious as airlines may automatically include features like travel insurance without confirming if you want them, so be sure to review your booking carefully.

Maintain Privacy

Maintaining anonymity during your flight ticket search process can be a crucial strategy for securing affordable fares. Flight ticket prices are often influenced by demand, with airlines using data on the number of people searching for specific tickets to adjust their prices accordingly. If you've noticed that the ticket price for a particular flight keeps increasing as you repeatedly check it, it's likely because the airline has identified your interest and aims to maximize profits. To counteract this, consider clearing your cookies and observe any changes in the ticket price once your browsing history has been cleared. This step can help you maintain a level playing field and potentially secure a better deal.

Sleeping in Comfort on a Budget

Stay in a Business Hotel

These budget-friendly and straightforward accommodations provide excellent rates for private rooms with attached amenities. You can find single rooms for as little as ¥6000 and double rooms starting as low as ¥8000, although prices may be slightly higher in major cities such as Tokyo, Osaka, and Kyoto. Keep an eye out for establishments that offer complimentary breakfasts—they often serve substantial meals that can keep you satisfied for hours.

A popular option in this category is none other than the Toyoko Inn, one of the biggest business hotel chains in Japan. The Toyoko Inn is known for its affordable rates, clean and comfortable rooms, and convenient locations near major transportation hubs and tourist attractions. With standard amenities, including private bathrooms, comfortable bedding, and free Wi-Fi, it offers a cost-effective option for travelers. Many branches provide complimentary breakfast and English-speaking staff to cater to international guests.

Sojourn in a Guesthouse or Hostel

Japan provides a wide array of exceptional guesthouses and hostels across the country, known for their extraordinary upkeep and cleanliness. In well-visited tourist regions, it's typical to come across welcoming staff proficient in English, acting as helpful guides akin to concierge services. While the facilities and rates for certain single or double rooms may resemble those of business hotels, the pricing for dormitory beds can differ. Nonetheless, it's common to discover options available at approximately ¥3000 (around $20). It's important to mention that you may occasionally find more budget-friendly rates when reserving directly with the establishment rather than using third-party booking platforms.

Nui. Hostel & Bar Lounge is an immensely popular choice among budget travelers. This hostel offers complimentary Wi-Fi and boasts a shared lounge area complete with a cafe and bar. It also provides guests with access to a communal kitchen. Each room has air conditioning, and each bed is furnished with a reading light, privacy curtain, and electric outlet.

Sleep in a Capsule Hotel in Urban Areas

Capsule hotels, known for their compact sleeping quarters that can accommodate just a bed, offer a cost-effective option for an overnight stay. While a capsule hotel may be a tad pricier than a dormitory bed at a hostel at around ¥4000 ($27) per night, the added privacy is a valuable perk. Particularly in cities where hotel rates tend to be on the higher side, capsules are an excellent choice for budget-conscious travelers looking to cut costs.

Budget travelers love making use of the 9 Hours capsule hotel chain located across Japan. The hotel offers guests a continental breakfast and complimentary Wi-Fi. It has air-conditioned rooms equipped with shared bathroom facilities and is entirely non-smoking. A reception desk that offers round-the-clock assistance and staff members proficient in both English and Japanese. It's important to note that this hotel offers dedicated areas exclusively for female guests. Travelers are advised to confirm the specific location when making their reservations.

Unforgettable Yet Affordable Activities

Hikes and Walking Tours

Hiking or trekking can be a cost-free and highly gratifying activity during your trip. You can explore emerging urban neighborhoods, traverse historic pilgrimage paths or countryside lanes, and venture into the mountains within Japan's national parks. You'll discover impressive architectural gems in Japanese cities designed by renowned Japanese architects.

Shrines and Temples

Most Shintō shrines in Japan don't require an entrance fee. Similarly, many temples allow visitors to explore their grounds at no cost, with charges typically applying only when entering specific halls or enclosed gardens.

Keeping Your Stomach and Wallet Full

Everything You Need and More at the Convenience Store

Japan boasts a wide array of dining options. While restaurants are aplenty, there's a particular culinary cornerstone deeply intertwined with the daily lives of Japanese people —the convenience store, affectionately known as "conbini." Dominated by major chains like Lawson, Family Mart, and 7-Eleven, these convenient havens are typically open 24/7, ensuring you can satiate your hunger at any hour. Moreover, you'll often find English labels on many food items, and a good number of store employees can speak English.

Convenience stores offer a wide range of culinary delights. Here's what you can expect to pay per item:

- **desserts:** ¥250-¥350 (around $1.70-$2.40)
- **drinks:** ¥110-¥250 (around $0.80-$1.70)
- **onigiri (rice ball):** ¥115-¥350 (around $0.80-$2.40)
- **sandwich:** ¥250-¥490 (around $1.70-$3.30)
- **salads:** ¥225-¥500 (around $1.50-$3.40)
- **steamed buns, deep-fried food, oden (a hearty stew of fish and vegetables), and other hot foods:** ¥150-¥600 (around $1-$4)
- **soba noodles and udon:** ¥400-¥660 (around $2.70-$4.40)

- **bentō boxes (boxed meals):** <¥1000 (around $6.80)

Fresh Food for Next to Nothing

Want to treat yourself to delicious Japanese food without breaking the bank? I may just have the solution for you. In most supermarkets, numerous fresh items are marked down after 7 p.m., with potential savings of up to 50% on select products. Typically, these discounted offerings include foods with a shorter shelf life, such as bentō, sushi, onigiri, and sashimi.

Utilizing Local Transportation

Japan Rail Pass

The Japan Rail Pass (JR Pass) provides unlimited access to all Shinkansen lines throughout the country. You can opt for a seven-day JR Pass, which is priced at ¥50,000 (around $337).

Regional-Specific Pass

Japan Rail (JR) provides a range of regional passes tailored for travel between specific destinations. Among these options, the Hokuriku Arch Pass stands out. While it does not cover the Tokaido Shinkansen, the high-speed rail link connecting Tokyo and Osaka, it does provide a scenic journey through the less-explored Hokuriku Region. The name "Arch Pass" comes from the route's arch-shaped trajectory. For travelers seeking alternatives to the traditional JR pass, the Hokuriku Arch Pass is a good choice, offering a seven-day pass priced at ¥24,500 (around $165).

Domestic One-Day Pass

If you find yourself primarily staying in one location, you might want to look into a domestic one-day pass. Tokyo's subway system, for example, offers a 24-hour pass priced at ¥800 (around $5.40) and a 72-hour pass for ¥1,500 (around $10.10) for adults. These passes provide convenient options for getting around and exploring the city without any hassle.

These cost-saving tactics will be explained in full in the following chapter, where we delve into the abundance of transportation options in Japan, helping you make the most of your budget while enjoying a seamless travel experience.

Now that you've got a handle on budget-friendly travel strategies let's shift our focus to staying connected without breaking the bank. In the upcoming section, we'll explore smart ways to access the internet inexpensively during your visit.

Accessing the Internet Inexpensively

Wi-Fi Hotspots

Travelers in Japan can conveniently access Wi-Fi at various public places, such as international airports, train stations, convenience stores, and coffee shops. NTT introduced the Japan Wi-Fi Auto-Connect app in 2019 to streamline this process, offering comprehensive coverage of free Wi-Fi locations tailored specifically for international tourists. This app is compatible with both iPhone and Android devices.

Rather than the traditional approach of individually logging into each Wi-Fi network, users only need to register once with the app. After the initial registration, your smartphone will automatically detect nearby Wi-Fi hotspots and establish a connection with your selected network. If you find yourself outside the range of a hotspot, the app will guide you to the nearest one and then seamlessly connect your device.

Data SIM Card and Pocket Wi-Fi

While public Wi-Fi hotspots and the Japan Wi-Fi Auto-Connect app are convenient in urban areas, their coverage may be limited in rural regions. To ensure a more secure and reliable internet connection during your travels, you might want to consider using either a data SIM card or pocket Wi-Fi. Data SIM cards provide high-speed internet on your mobile phone without any contractual commitments, although they do not support regular calls or text messaging. On the other hand, pocket Wi-Fi is a portable router that creates a personal high-speed hotspot, accommodating multiple devices.

Japan hosts numerous providers of data SIM cards. As a point of reference, Mobal provides an eight-day unlimited data SIM card for around $32 and a 16-day option for around $43. You can order your chosen data SIM online and arrange to collect it on your specified date at predetermined locations, like the airport or your hotel. Some even offer data eSIM cards for added convenience.

For group travelers, pocket Wi-Fi might prove to be the most cost-effective option. Like data SIM cards, several companies offer Wi-Fi routers. To obtain one, simply place an order on the chosen provider's website and specify your pickup and return dates. Depending on the company, you can either collect and return the routers at the airport or opt for direct delivery to your hotel. It's worth noting that some providers facilitate returns at specific spots, while others may require you to mail the router back. For price reference, Ninja Wi-Fi's unlimited 5G-per-day plan costs around $7.35 per day, and their 10G-per-day option is around $8.80 per day.

As we've covered staying connected on a budget, now let's shift our focus to experiencing the more luxurious side of

Japan with upscale accommodations and traditional ryokan experiences.

INDULGING IN LUXURY ACCOMMODATIONS AND ENCHANTING RYOKANS

Luxury Hotels

Luxury hotels in Japan offer an exceptional blend of modern elegance and meticulous service, creating a lavish and memorable experience for discerning travelers. These hotels often boast stunning architectural designs, awe-inspiring views, and meticulously crafted interiors. From the towering skyscrapers of Tokyo to the serene ryokan-inspired retreats in the countryside, Japan's luxury hotels cater to a wide range of tastes.

Guests can expect world-class dining, opulent spa treatments, and personalized attention to detail. Many of these hotels seamlessly combine contemporary amenities with traditional Japanese aesthetics, ensuring a harmonious and luxurious stay that showcases the country's renowned hospitality.

While well-established international hotel chains such as Hyatt Regency and Four Seasons are synonymous with luxury, Japan's hidden treasure is the HOSHINOYA Luxury Hotels. Operating in both urban and rural settings throughout Japan, this brand offers a collection of luxury sub-brands, including Hoshinoya, Kai, and Risonare. The Hoshinoya sub-brand epitomizes the pinnacle of luxury accommodations, while Kai is celebrated for its locations in traditional hot spring areas. In contrast, Risonare celebrates the charm of countryside resort hotels with a focus on the unique culinary culture of each region.

Yet, Hoshinoya Luxury Hotels go beyond mere aesthetic allure. They seamlessly weave themselves into local traditions, cultures, and the ever-changing beauty of the seasons, ensuring that guests experience a transformative journey as they immerse themselves in this world of awe and wonder.

Ryokans

A ryokan is a quintessential Japanese inn that embodies traditional hospitality, offering a unique and immersive experience for travelers seeking an authentic taste of Japan's rich culture. Staying in a ryokan is akin to stepping back in time, where guests can expect tatami-matted rooms, sliding paper doors, and futon bedding.

The serene and tranquil atmosphere is often surrounded by picturesque natural settings like hot springs or gardens. Staying in a Ryokan is a peaceful and contemplative way to connect with Japanese customs and traditions, making it a truly memorable and culturally enriching experience.

Situated approximately two and a half hours away from Tokyo by train, Lake Kawaguchiko is home to one of the finest onsen Ryokan experiences at the Fuji Kawaguchiko Onsen Hotel Konansou. What sets this establishment apart is not only its commitment to preserving Japanese tradition but also its stunning vistas. From the comfort of your room to the soothing natural hot spring baths, you'll have the privilege of savoring uninterrupted and awe-inspiring views of both the majestic Mount Fuji and the serene Kawaguchiko landscape. It's a setting that beautifully complements the rich cultural experience you'll encounter during your stay.

TO SUMMARIZE

In this chapter, we went over the following:

- cost estimation
- top places to exchange currency
- tips for budget travelers
- luxury accommodations and ryokans

With your budget set, it's time to implement these financial strategies. With a well-organized travel budget spreadsheet and a clear vision of your financial priorities, you'll embark on your Japan adventure well-prepared and with peace of mind.

In the following chapter, we'll dive into one of the most essential aspects of traveling in Japan—navigating the transportation system. We'll explore the ins and outs of Japan's efficient, reliable, and sometimes perplexing transportation network.

3

NAVIGATING JAPAN'S TRANSPORTATION SYSTEM

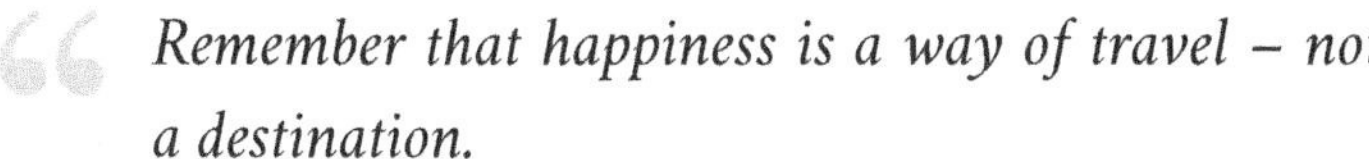

> *Remember that happiness is a way of travel – not a destination.*
>
> — ROY M. GOODMAN

AN OVERVIEW OF JAPAN'S PUBLIC TRANSPORT

While Japan's geographical isolation may present initial travel challenges, once you set foot on this beautiful island nation, your journey through the country couldn't be more convenient. Japan's remarkable public transportation system is your gateway to seamlessly navigating sprawling cities and charming villages. From the high-speed marvel of the shinkansen to the humble yet efficient local trains, their schedules are followed with an almost religious devotion—so punctual you could set your watch by them. Even local buses and long-distance coaches maintain this precision, and the fleet of spotlessly clean taxis that grace the streets is both reliable and trustworthy, making your exploration of Japan a smooth and enjoyable experience.

Rail Transit

JR Shinkansen

You're in for a treat as you explore Japan's vibrant landscape! The country's primary islands—Honshu, Kyushu, and Hokkaido—are seamlessly connected by a remarkable web of high-speed train lines, all radiating from Tokyo to major cities throughout Japan. These high-speed wonders, affectionately known as "shinkansen," are run by the trusted Japan Railways (JR).

Zooming along at speeds of up to 200 mph, the Shinkansen is renowned for several fantastic qualities that make your journey an absolute breeze, including impeccable punctuality, with most trains departing at their scheduled times and not a second later. Plus, you'll be traveling in style and comfort, with seats that always face forward and whisper-quiet cabins—ideal for taking in those picturesque views. Safety is paramount, and the Shinkansen boasts an impeccable record with no fatal accidents in its entire history. As if that weren't enough, you'll find that the efficiency of these trains is nothing short of impressive.

Within the expansive Shinkansen network, you'll discover a variety of lines, with the Tokaido Shinkansen (connecting Osaka, Kyoto, Nagoya, and Tokyo) standing as both the eldest and most beloved. Almost all Shinkansen lines (excluding the Yamagata and Akita Shinkansen) boast dedicated tracks exclusively for these high-speed trains. What's remarkable is that most lines offer multiple train categories, spanning from the slowest category that makes stops at every station along the way to the swiftest category with stops only at major stations.

JR Trains

Japan's reputation for its incredibly efficient train network is well-deserved. However, it's understandable that with so many lines connecting various cities and neighborhoods, the whole system might seem like a tangled web. However, I'm here to unravel it for you! Let's go over everything you need to know.

Firstly, 80% of Japan's extensive rail system is overseen by a group known as JR, or Japan Railways Group, consisting of six regional companies, each managing train services in their respective areas. These six regional companies are:

1. Hokkaido Railway Company (JR Hokkaido)
2. East Japan Railway Company (JR East)
3. West Japan Railway Company (JR West)
4. Central Japan Railway Company (JR Central)
5. Shikoku Railway Company (JR Shikoku)

6. Kyushu Railway Company (JR Kyushu)

Within JR's extensive network of conventional lines, you'll encounter four primary types of trains, each with its unique characteristics:

Local

Local trains are your reliable companions for everyday commuting and short rides when you need to get from one part of a city to another. The Yamanote Line in Tokyo is a well-known example of a local train service. It forms a loop around the city, stopping at key stations like Ikebukuro, Shinjuku, Shibuya, and Tokyo, making it an excellent choice for both tourists and locals looking to visit Tokyo's major hubs. A complete trip around the Yamanote Line typically takes around an hour, providing a convenient way to navigate the heart of the city.

Rapid

Rapid trains, a variation of local trains, predominantly operate in major cities and their surroundings, including vibrant metropolises like Tokyo, Osaka, and Nagoya. These trains are designed to swiftly transport passengers between key stations, making them an efficient choice for daily commuters. In cities like Tokyo and Osaka, you'll find even faster Rapid services known as "Special Rapid Service" trains, ensuring an even faster transit for busy city dwellers. A great example of a rapid train is the Chuo Line in Tokyo (or JR Central Line), which runs a nearly straight route through the heart of Tokyo, stopping at crucial stations like Shinjuku, Akihabara, and Tokyo Station.

Limited Express

Limited express trains represent the swiftest mode of travel on JR conventional railway lines in Japan. With over 100 distinct types of limited express trains criss-crossing the nation, they play a vital role in connecting major cities and regions that lie beyond the reach of the Shinkansen network. Additionally, express trains, albeit not as fast as the Shinkansen, halt at key stations, making them an excellent choice for airport transfers. Notable examples include the Tokyo Monorail, which provides access to Haneda International Airport, the Narita Express (N'EX) serving Narita International Airport, and the Haruka Express, which offers quick transport to Kansai International Airport.

Joyful

When you step onto a joyful train, you're not merely embarking on a mode of transportation; you're entering a realm of pure delight. These extraordinary trains redefine travel, turning the journey itself into a destination.

A popular joyful train is one that was introduced in 2012 to uplift local spirits after a devastating earthquake and tsunami. The POKÉMON with YOU Train is a fun and heartwarming creation that brings a touch of magic to your travel. Pikachu, the beloved Pokémon character, adorns both the exterior and interior, creating a whimsical atmosphere. Inside, you'll discover two enchanting Pikachu-themed cars. The "Playroom Car" is a haven for kids and the young at heart. With many small Pikachu plushies and a prominent Pikachu plushie at the center, there's no shortage of adorable company. A small ball pit, headbands, accessories, and even mini conductor hats allow for endless fun.

Private Trains

It's not just JR that keeps Japan's trains running on time. The remaining 20% of rail services are provided by numerous private railway companies, particularly in and around bustling metropolitan areas. In most major cities and their adjacent regions, you'll find prominent private railway companies that boast extensive networks. These private lines frequently crisscross with the JR routes but also extend their services to regions that are not yet covered by JR lines.

For example, the Fujikyuko Line is the preferred rail route to reach the iconic Mount Fuji. This train line efficiently transports passengers to Kawaguchiko Station, the primary station on the northern side of Mount Fuji. From Kawaguchiko train station, you'll have easy access not only to the mountain itself but also to attractions like the Fuji-Q Highland amusement park and Lake Kawaguchi.

Subways

While JR Trains is fantastic for traveling across Japan, its coverage within major cities is more limited. In bustling urban hubs like Tokyo and Osaka, the subway networks are your go-to mode of transportation for city exploration. For instance, in Tokyo, you'll find two primary operators of subway lines: Tokyo Metro and Toei.

Navigating the Tokyo subway is a breeze. At every station, you'll encounter ticket machines with multilingual options. You can either purchase a one-way fare ticket or opt for a rechargeable IC card to easily glide through the ticket gates. Additionally, Tokyo Metro and Toei offer tourists a convenient subway pass, saving you some yen during your travels.

If you're planning to make multiple subway trips within a few days, consider getting a tourist pass for unlimited travel on all subway lines. You can choose from 72-hour, 48-hour, or 24-hour options. These passes can be obtained from select subway stations, Tokyo Metro Pass Offices, major electronics stores like Bic Camera, and various tourist information centers across the city. Make sure to bring your passport to show that you're a visitor to Japan.

In Osaka, subways and the Osaka Loop Line (operated by JR West) are your best companions for getting around the city. While it may not be as extensive as Tokyo's subway, it provides excellent coverage throughout the city.

Payment methods in Osaka are straightforward. You can use IC cards, which can be easily purchased within the city. Alternatively, you have the option to buy single tickets or take advantage of one of Osaka's convenient day passes, such as the Osaka One-Day Pass—Enjoy Eco Card. With this pass, you can enjoy unlimited rides on the Osaka City Bus and all Osaka Metro lines for one day. It's priced at ¥820 (around $5.50) for adults on weekdays and ¥620 (around $4.15) on weekends and holidays.

Buses

Visitors commonly overlook the convenience and cost-effectiveness of bus travel when connecting to different destinations. Depending on your specific destination, bus journeys can sometimes not only be more convenient but also shorter than train rides, especially when you can avoid the hassle of train transfers. Additionally, buses provide essential access to places that may not have train services, including the more remote areas of the Northern Japanese Alps around Takayama or picturesque villages like Shirakawa-go in Gifu.

Buses in Japan can be divided into two main categories: local and long-distance. Let's review what each entails and where you can expect to go with them.

Local Bus Networks

In major urban centers like Tokyo, Osaka, and certain other large cities, buses are supplementary to the public transportation system, providing additional options alongside the train and subway networks. However, in cities with less extensive train infrastructure, such as Kyoto, buses take on the primary role of public transportation. Furthermore, buses are vital for connecting rural areas, smaller towns, and national parks. Most buses typically allow payments in both cash and IC cards. Carrying a rechargeable IC card like Suica or Pasmo can be incredibly convenient for your bus travels throughout Japan.

Long-Distance Buses

Japan boasts an expansive network of long-distance highway buses (kōsoku buses) that effectively link various regions across the country. Certain highway buses even offer overnight travel options. While they may not be as swift as the Shinkansen, highway buses are often a budget-friendly choice. Keep in mind that most highway buses do require advance seat reservations, although not all of them can be reserved online in English.

Taxis

Taxis in Japan are known for their cleanliness, top-notch service, and, yes, their relatively higher fares. Hailing a taxi in Japan is quite similar to the process in Western countries. You can either head to a taxi stand and patiently wait for one, flag down a passing taxi on the street, call a taxi company for a pick-up, or use one of the popular taxi-hailing apps like GO, DIDI, and Uber.

Many taxis in Japan offer the convenience of payment by credit card, and an increasing number of them also accept IC cards, with the accepted payment methods typically indicated by stickers on the taxi's door. When settling your fare with cash, avoid paying small amounts with large bills, as it might be inconvenient for the driver. Additionally, don't tip your driver as this will cause them the additional inconvenience of chasing after you to give you your money back. We'll discuss Japan's no-tipping culture in the next chapter.

As for the fare structure, when you hop into a standard four-passenger taxi, the initial fare is usually between ¥400–¥750 (around $2.70–$5.00) for the first mile. Beyond this, expect an increase of ¥80–¥100 (around $0.55–$0.70) for every additional 220–400 yards traveled. The fare may also rise if the taxi remains stationary for an extended period. If your taxi journey includes the use of expressways, the corresponding expressway tolls will be added to your total fare.

Here are a few handy tips to keep in mind when using taxis in Japan:

Don't Get a Taxi From the Airport

Except for Fukuoka Airport, which is conveniently located less than five minutes from the city center, taking a taxi from the airport in any other Japanese city is generally not recommended. This is due to taxi drivers attracting tourists from airports such as Narita. Traveling from Narita Airport to Shinjuku typically takes around one hour and is estimated to cost approximately ¥31,476 (around $210).

Taxis Get Extremely Expensive Between 10 p.m. and 5 a.m.

During the late evening hours, usually between 10 p.m. and 5 a.m., taxi fares are commonly subject to a 20% increase. If you happen to be a considerable distance from home after the last train, I recommend taking a nap at an internet cafe, which typically provides mattresses, and waiting for the first train. By employing this approach, especially if your location is more than an hour away from your hotel or place of residence, you could save approximately ¥10,000 (around $67).

Avoid Getting a Taxi at Rush Hour

During Tokyo's rush hour, the road traffic comes to a virtual standstill. In the majority of situations, even if Google Maps suggests that taking a taxi might be quicker, it is advisable to opt for the subway or train. These alternatives are not only more cost-effective but also faster and more convenient.

THE CONVENIENCE AND VALUE OF JAPAN RAIL PASSES

Introducing the Japan Rail Pass

The Japan Rail Pass (JR Pass) is a nationwide travel pass designed for long-distance train journeys within Japan. This pass is exclusively available to foreign tourists and provides unlimited access to JR trains for durations of one, two, or three weeks. This pass grants unrestricted access to all JR public transportation options, including shinkansen, JR lines mentioned above, ferries, JR buses, and airport transfers.

Prior to October 2023, the cost of a seven-day JR Pass was ¥29,650 (around $200). To put this in perspective, a round-trip ticket from Tokyo to Kyoto typically costs around ¥28,340 (around $190), and most visitors spend between ¥4,000 and ¥8,000 (around $26.90 to $53.70) on local trains and buses in a week. However, following a significant price increase in autumn 2023, it's now more cost-effective to purchase individual point-to-point train tickets for a trip primarily encompassing Tokyo, Osaka, and Kyoto, as opposed to opting for a seven-day JR Pass.

Nonetheless, the JR Pass retains its value for those planning to explore multiple cities on a round trip. It streamlines the ticketing process, eliminating the need to acquire separate tickets for each destination. This convenience proves especially advantageous when navigating Japan's intricate railway system or if you happen to find yourself on the wrong platform. With a JR Pass, there's no need to purchase additional tickets; you can readily use your JR Pass to secure new tickets for your desired train. In instances where no reservation is required, you can simply display your JR Pass to board the train.

Another change in the JR Pass is that it now covers the Nozomi and Mizuho trains on the Tokaido and Sanyo Shinkansen Lines upon purchasing a special ticket. You'll still have access to the Hikari or Sakura services that cover the same routes, reaching the same top speed as the Nozomi and Mizuho trains but making more stops along each route. For instance, from Tokyo to Kyoto, the Hikari takes 15 minutes longer than the equivalent Nozomi.

Furthermore, if your travel itinerary focuses on exploring eastern Japan and you wish to experience the joyful trains, consider the JR EAST PASS (Tohoku area) priced at ¥30,000 (around $200) or the JR EAST PASS (Nagano, Niigata area) available for ¥27,000 (around $181). These passes offer attractive alternatives for your journey.

Lastly, it's important to note that the JR Pass does not cover subways, buses (with exceptions for JR buses bearing a JR logo), and private railway lines.

How to Purchase, Activate, and Use a JR Pass

You can acquire a JR Pass Exchange Order via the official JR Pass website (japanrailpass.net) or through authorized distributors like jrpass.com or Klook.com. For the convenience of obtaining your pass, you can check for nearby overseas JR-designated sales offices or agencies on the official JR Pass website. If you have one near you, you have the option to call, purchase, and collect your JR Pass Exchange Order directly from their office.

Opting for an online purchase involves a straightforward process of following a few simple steps and confirming your online order. Thereafter, the Exchange Order will be dispatched to you by mail. You have the choice of having it delivered to your residence before your departure or to your accommodation in Japan.

Various websites offer different delivery times, spanning from 48 hours to five days. To ensure a hassle-free experience, it's advisable to place your order for the JR Pass Exchange Order at least two to three weeks before your intended travel date, particularly during peak holiday seasons. Please note that starting from October 1, 2023, the JR Pass will no longer be available for purchase within Japan. Additionally, remember that the validation and exchange of your order for the actual pass must be completed within 90 days of purchase. Therefore, it's most suitable to purchase your Japan Rail Pass no more than 90 days before your intended exchange date.

To activate your JR Pass, simply visit any of the JR Exchange offices located at airport terminals, metro stations, or train stations with your JR Exchange Order and passport. Ensure that you present the original Exchange Order document, as photocopies are not accepted. At the exchange office, you can specify the start date you prefer for your JR Pass, and the staff will assist you accordingly.

Now that you're familiar with the activation process for your JR Pass, it's equally important to understand how to use it effectively at train stations in Japan. When you're at a station, simply locate the automated gates designated for JR stations. In cases where such gates are unavailable, you can head to the ticket booth and present your pass there. After completing either of these processes, you'll be ready to proceed to your platform and enjoy seamless train travel throughout Japan.

Secure Your Spot With Easy Seat Reservation

Most bullet trains offer both non-reserved and reserved seats in separate cars. Typically, there are plenty of empty, non-reserved seats. However, train carriages can become noticeably crowded during holiday periods or peak commuting times. If you're contemplating seat reservations, remember that you are not obliged to secure seat reservations for local or rapid lines such as the Chuo Line and Yamanote Loop Line. On the other hand, it's important to note that nearly all joyful train lines necessitate seat reservations and tickets for boarding. With a JR Pass, you can reserve seats on all JR trains, including Shinkansen, at no extra cost to facilitate your boarding process.

To secure your seat reservations, visit the ticket offices identified by their distinctive green sign, known as Midori-no-madoguchi, or head to Travel Service Centres and JR-affiliated Travel Agencies.

Here's a step-by-step guide for reserving your seats:

1. Bring your Japan Rail Pass to the Midori-no-madoguchi.
2. Indicate your preferred train and whether you prefer a smoking or non-smoking area.
3. Receive your reserved seat ticket.
4. Display your Japan Rail Pass at the ticket gate and proceed to your designated platform.
5. Retain your ticket, as you may be required to present both your Japan Rail Pass and your seat reservation to the ticket inspector.
6. Take your seats and enjoy the ride!

USE IC CARDS FOR SEAMLESS TRAVEL ACROSS DIFFERENT MODES OF TRANSPORTATION

IC cards have come up a few times thus far, so you might be curious about what they actually are. In a nutshell, IC cards are convenient, prepaid, and reloadable smart cards designed for seamless payments for public transportation systems and quick touch-based transactions for vending machines and convenience stores.

IC cards are so appealing because they are user-friendly, simplifying electronic payments by enabling you to effortlessly tap them on card readers, especially when using public transportation. With IC cards, you can say goodbye to the trouble of navigating ticket machines to figure out the right trains or subways, calculating fares, and painstakingly inputting the exact amount of money for your tickets.

Japan offers a variety of IC cards, with Pasmo and Suica being the primary players. Suica and PASMO cards are completely interchangeable, so you can use either card wherever they are accepted. Your choice of card may depend on where you are buying it. If you're at a JR station, consider buying a Suica card, but if you're at a subway or private railway station, opt for a PASMO card.

TIPS FOR EFFICIENT AND COST-EFFECTIVE TRAVEL

Use Smartphone Apps for Real-Time Transportation Schedules and Route Planning

It's normal to feel nervous about navigating Japan's array of transportation options. However, fear not; there's a variety of apps available to assist you in this aspect. With their help, you'll be traversing Japan like a pro. Let's look at a few of these apps and how they can help you.

Japan Travel

In Japan, Navitime is renowned for its automated trip planning feature, which compiles various train routes based on your specified date and time of travel. Their app, "Japan Travel," is no exception and even takes into account any tourist passes you might have, making it particularly valuable if you're using the Japan Rail Pass to maximize its benefits.

What sets this Japan train app apart is its ability to create customized itineraries and provide detailed English maps for tourists, showcasing a wide range of useful locations. Searching for nearby stores or services is effortless – just tap the corresponding icon at the bottom of the screen, whether it's restaurants, convenience stores, or ATMs, and watch the pins for these locations appear on the map.

Additionally, the itinerary function allows you to store your entire trip plan in one place conveniently. However, some features are restricted to paid users, but essential functions like the map and train route planner are entirely free to use.

Japan Transit Planner

This app offers comprehensive details such as distance, fares, seat types (reserved or non-reserved), and any applicable surcharges for train journeys. It also provides information on trip durations and total costs, with the added feature of filtering out services that the Japan Rail Pass does not cover.

Google Maps

Over the past decade, Google Maps has undergone significant enhancements, emerging as one of the premier travel apps for navigating Japan and beyond. It not only facilitates seamless navigation but also offers comprehensive information on various locations throughout Japan.

This extensive coverage spans a wide spectrum, encompassing everything from restaurants and businesses to popular tourist attractions. In essence, it serves as a versatile trip-planning tool that consolidates essential details in one place.

One standout feature is Street View, which proves invaluable for travelers. The ability to zoom into the streets alleviates any uncertainty during your travels in Japan. Gone are the days of pondering, "Is this the correct location?" With Google Maps, you can visually confirm your destination's appearance, whether it's a landmark, a station, or the front of a hotel or restaurant.

Furthermore, if you encounter situations where internet access is unavailable, there's no need to fret. Google Maps offers offline functionality in Japan, provided you prepare in advance by downloading the necessary maps.

Take Advantage of Exclusive Discounts and Deals for Tourists

While the Japan Rail Pass caters to foreign travelers seeking nationwide coverage, there exists a range of special tourist discount passes tailored to those who wish to immerse themselves deeply in a specific region or city. These specialized discount passes are designed to facilitate unlimited use of designated modes of transportation within a particular area.

By consolidating fares, these passes spare travelers the hassle of purchasing multiple tickets throughout the day and are available in various validity periods. Let's review these passes and their suitability for different types of travelers.

Greater Tokyo Pass

The Greater Tokyo Pass presents an attractive choice for travelers looking to explore Tokyo and the renowned tourist attractions in the neighboring prefectures of Chiba, Saitama, and Kanagawa. This pass gives you access to an extensive web of private railways and bus routes, giving you the freedom of unlimited travel over five days. It's quite affordable, too, with a cost of ¥7,200 (around $48) for adults. There's also a three-day option priced at ¥6,000 (around $40.30) for adults. Please note that the three-day pass exclusively grants access to private railway lines and doesn't include bus services. So, you can explore to your heart's content, all within the time frame that suits your journey.

Apart from the Greater Tokyo Pass, numerous other discounted transportation passes are at your disposal to facilitate cost-effective travel within the Tokyo region, namely:

- Keisei Skyliner & Tokyo Subway Ticket (1, 2, or 3-Day Pass)
- Tokyo 1-Day Ticket (1-Day Pass)
- JR Tokyo Wide Pass (3-Day Pass)

Kansai Thru Pass

The Kansai Thru Pass is an excellent choice if you plan to explore the areas around Kyoto and Osaka, including Kobe, Nara, Asuka, Koyasan, Himeji, and Wakayama. It provides unlimited travel on buses, subways, and trains, except for JR trains, within the Kansai region. The pass offers two-day options, with prices starting at ¥4,380 (around $30) for two days and ¥5,400 (around $36) for three days, and there's a 50% discount for children aged six to twelve.

You can use the pass on non-consecutive days during its validity period, and it comes in a ticket form that can be inserted into automatic ticket gates. Since cities like Kyoto and Nara rely on non-JR railways, the Kansai Thru Pass is particularly advantageous for urban travel, and it becomes even more economical when combined with day trips to destinations like Wakayama, Shin-Kobe, and Himeji, which are also covered by the pass.

Visit Hiroshima Tourist Pass

The Visit Hiroshima Tourist Pass provides travelers with unlimited access to various modes of transportation within Hiroshima. It covers all Hiroshima Electric Railway Hiroden streetcars within the city, bus routes operated by six bus companies in the central area of Hiroshima City, and includes ferry rides to Miyajima island, famous for the iconic Itsukushima Shrine. The one-day pass is priced at ¥1000 (around $6.70), the two-day pass at ¥1500 (around $10), and the three-day pass at ¥2000 (around $13.)

IN SUMMARY

In this chapter, we explored the following topics:

- an overview of Japan's public transport
- the convenience and value of rail passes
- the value of IC Cards for seamless travel across different modes of transportation
- tips for efficient and cost-effective travel

With the convenience of Japan's efficient transportation system, you can easily immerse yourself in cultural gems. For example, when stepping off the train in Kyoto, you're immediately surrounded by Japan's rich history and culture, with ancient temples and serene zen gardens awaiting your exploration. In the next chapter, we'll guide you through the local customs, etiquette, and traditions that each of these cultural gems hold, and what makes Japan a unique and unforgettable destination.

4

DIVE INTO JAPAN'S CULTURAL TAPESTRY

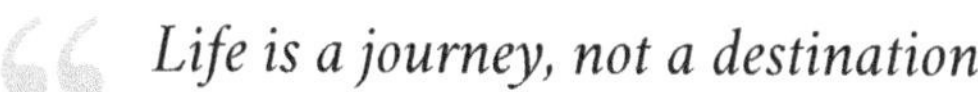

> *Life is a journey, not a destination.*
>
> — RALPH WALDO EMERSON

Traveling to Japan offers more than just the chance to visit iconic landmarks; it's a journey of immersion into their rich culture and traditions that have shaped this captivating country for centuries. Every moment in Japan is an opportunity to embrace the heart and soul of a nation where past and present coexist harmoniously.

ETIQUETTE AND CULTURAL NORMS TO BE AWARE OF

Bowing Etiquette: When and How to Bow

In Japan, bowing serves as a nuanced form of expression, conveying a spectrum of emotions such as gratitude, remorse, respect, or appreciation. This customary gesture is typically categorized into two distinct styles: standing, referred to as "ritsurei," and kneeling, known as "zarei." In either form, it's essential to maintain an upright posture, keeping your back straight while bending at the waist.

Occasions That Require Bowing

Bowing transcends mere greetings in Japan; it holds significance in various contexts, including:

- bidding farewell
- initiating training sessions
- demonstrating respect
- offering congratulations
- conveying profound gratitude
- seeking a favor
- showing appreciation
- extending apologies
- commencing formal ceremonies
- expressing sympathy
- when entering or leaving a martial arts dojo

Deciding Whether to Shake Hands or Bow

During initial encounters, it's common for Japanese individuals to opt for a handshake when meeting Westerners to avoid potential awkwardness. When in Japan, it's advisable to follow the lead of your hosts regarding whether to initiate a handshake or a bow. If someone offers a bow, it's essential to reciprocate respectfully. Japanese hosts are well-versed in preserving the dignity of all involved and will strive to prevent any uncomfortable situations. While handshakes remain relatively infrequent among Japanese people, they have come to symbolize a profound bond, signifying a deeper connection than the casual handshakes often seen in Western culture.

Shaking Hands and Bowing Simultaneously

To avoid the common mistake newcomers make of inadvertently bowing when the other party intends to shake hands, it's essential to clearly communicate your intention. If the other person extends their hand for a handshake, refrain from initiating a bow. You can usually anticipate whether a person or group plans to bow first as you approach each other. They tend to stop at a slightly greater distance, just beyond handshake range, with their feet together. Following the bow, you can then close the gap with a step or two and proceed to shake hands if necessary.

While it's possible for both a bow and a handshake to occur simultaneously, it's generally considered better etiquette to perform them separately. Maintaining solid eye contact is expected during a handshake, whereas, during a proper bow, the customary practice is to lower your gaze. In the event of a combination bow and handshake, you'll likely find yourselves in close proximity. Remember to turn slightly to your left to prevent an accidental head bump.

How to Bow Correctly

The proper way to bow involves several key elements. Begin by bending at the waist while maintaining a straight back and neck, with your feet together. Keep your arms straight at your sides during the bow. For women, it's common to bow with their fingertips together or their hands clasped in front at thigh level. As you bow, your gaze should be directed downward, looking at the ground.

The depth and duration of the bow convey the level of respect and submission. A quick, informal bow typically involves a bend of around 15 degrees, whereas a more formal bow requires bending the torso to approximately a 30-degree angle. The deepest bow, demonstrating the utmost respect, involves bending to a full 45 degrees while keeping your eyes on your shoes. Holding the bow for a while further emphasizes respect. In general, it's customary to offer deeper bows to individuals in positions of authority, elders, judges, or those of higher rank or office, as well as in situations where additional respect is warranted.

In some instances, you may find yourself engaged in a series of bows until one party eventually concludes the ritual. Subsequent bows tend to be less deep than the initial ones. When bowing in crowded or confined spaces, it's advisable to turn slightly to your left to avoid inadvertent head collisions with others.

Following the exchange of bows, it's customary to reciprocate with friendly eye contact and a warm smile. Ideally, avoid combining a bow, which entails looking downward, with a handshake, as handshakes typically require maintaining eye contact.

Taking Off Your Shoes Indoors

Removing your shoes as you step inside is a meaningful gesture in Japan, signifying your respect for the space you're about to enter. Taking off your shoes is considered customary etiquette, especially when you spot a tatami mat near the entrance of a building. This conveys your reverence for the environment you're entering and distinctly marks the boundary between the outside world and the interior space.

Show Kindness to Your Feet

Footwear, particularly Western-style shoes, can often feel quite confining for your feet. The custom of taking off your shoes indoors, particularly at home, is a way of showing respect and care for your feet. This practice is especially prevalent in places of leisure and relaxation, such as Japanese inns, hotels, and spas, where it aligns with the overall ambiance and allows your feet to relax and breathe freely.

The Importance of Cleanliness

Cleanliness is highly esteemed in Japan, and people take great pride in maintaining a spotless living environment. As a result, it's customary to remove your shoes and often wear the slippers provided when entering a Japanese home.

Tradition and Respect at Japanese Temples

When you step into the sacred grounds of a Japanese temple or shrine, the practice of removing your shoes is not just a mere tradition; it's a deeply ingrained sign of respect. It's essential to remember this cultural custom when planning future trips to Japan or considering events at such locations.

Proper Conduct at Temples and Shrines

Entering A Shrine

When you step into a Shinto shrine in Japan, you'll notice that many visitors bow as a sign of respect. It's a beautiful gesture that reflects the deep cultural traditions of the country.

However, there's a custom you should be aware of to avoid unintentional disrespect. As you approach the shrine, take care not to walk down the center path under the torii or Shinto gate. This path is reserved exclusively for the shrine's deity; only the god of the shrine can pass through it. So, when visiting these sacred places, it's essential to stay to the side and show your respect in other ways, such as bowing or making an offering.

Preparing Through Purification

Before engaging in prayer at a Japanese shrine, worshippers typically begin by purifying themselves at the temizuya or chozuya, a special fountain or stone basin filled with water. This ritual is an essential part of the Shinto tradition.

Here's how it works: You'll find a wooden ladle near the temizuya. First, use it to scoop water into your left hand, then your right. Afterward, scoop water into your left hand once more and use it to rinse your mouth. This symbolic act is a way of physically and spiritually cleansing yourself before entering the shrine's sacred space.

Offering Prayers at the Shrine

When it comes to offering prayers at a Japanese shrine, there are certain customs and rituals to observe. Typically, worshippers stand in front of the honden, the main hall where the kami (deity) resides. Here's a step-by-step guide to this sacred practice:

- **Make an offering:** Begin by placing a coin in the offering box. Five-yen coins are considered particularly auspicious, as their name, "go-en," sounds like the word for "luck" in Japanese.
- **Ring the bell:** If you see a bell hanging above the offering box, use the attached rope to ring it gently. This act is believed to alert the kami to your presence and your intentions.
- **Clap and bow:** Perform two bows and then clap twice. This is a sign of respect and a way to gain the kami's attention.
- **State your prayers:** Take a moment to silently offer your prayers and express your wishes to the kami.
- **Bow once more:** To conclude your ritual, bow once more as a sign of gratitude.

Additionally, visitors have the option to write down their petitions on small wooden tablets known as ema. After inscribing their wishes, these ema tablets are often hung on a designated tree or pegboard near the main hall.

Gift-Giving Culture in Japan

When it comes to gift-giving in Japan, adhering to cultural traditions is essential. Here are some key customs to keep in mind:

- Present and accept gifts using both hands as a gesture of respect.
- When receiving a gift, it's customary to initially decline it, often up to three times, before ultimately accepting it. This humble gesture shows appreciation.
- Avoid giving gifts to only one individual when you're in a group setting. It's considered impolite. Instead, consider offering something to the entire group.
- Opening a gift in front of a large audience is generally seen as rude. Therefore, refrain from opening gifts until you're home or at another private place.
- Don't rush to present gifts at the beginning of a meeting or encounter. Instead, offering them at the end of the interaction is more appropriate, as doing so is considered polite and respectful of the occasion.

By adhering to these customs, you'll not only show respect for Japanese traditions but also enhance your interactions and relationships in this rich culture.

Onsen Culture

When enjoying the serene experience of an onsen, it's crucial to adhere to traditional manners and etiquette:

- **au naturel soak:** Embrace the tradition of bathing nude – no swimsuits allowed.
- **hygiene first:** Prior to entering the onsen, ensure you're immaculately clean. A thorough wash in the designated shower is a must.
- **considerate washing:** When washing or showering, be mindful of fellow bathers' space and comfort.
- **no need for speed:** Maintain a calm demeanor—running and swimming inside the onsen area are discouraged.
- **stay sober:** This rule is in place to keep you safe since the combination of hot water and alcohol can lead to dehydration very quickly. Therefore, abstain from alcohol prior to your onsen experience.
- **glass-free zone:** Keep glass items outside the onsen area to prevent accidents.
- **no bathing in the bath:** Refrain from using soap or shampoo inside the bathtub– the onsen is for soaking only.
- **towel-free soak:** Keep your towel out of the onsen water.

- **pre-exit pat down:** Before leaving the onsen area, dry your body.

By acknowledging these onsen customs, you'll not only respect the age-old traditions but also ensure a harmonious experience for everyone. Enjoy your soak!

No Tipping Culture

Tipping in Japan is not a customary practice, and efforts to leave a tip will likely be politely declined, potentially resulting in an awkward situation. In Japan, the thought is that when you dine out or enjoy drinks at a bar, you already compensate the establishment for their quality service. Whether at a humble ramen shop or a lavish hotel, you can expect attentive, thoughtful service without any expectation of gratuity. If you're accustomed to tipping practices in other countries, it might initially feel unusual not to leave a small tip, but it's simply not a custom in Japan.

Vending Machine Culture

In modern-day Japan, a vast network of vending machines offers a diverse array of products and services, spanning from coffee, bananas, ramen, ice cream, shampoo, T-shirts, batteries, and umbrellas. You can even purchase a shot of restorative oxygen if needed. Whether you need a last-minute bouquet of flowers or you've forgotten to don a tie for the office, rest assured that somewhere, there's a vending machine ready to assist you.

Few Trash Cans

In Japan, causing inconvenience to others or disrupting societal harmony often warrants an apology, even in seemingly minor situations from an outsider's perspective. Consequently, Japanese individuals are notably conscientious about public spaces and their personal conduct within them. They understand that public spaces belong to the collective, so maintaining cleanliness becomes a shared responsibility.

As a result, a profound cultural norm in Japan emphasizes the upkeep of public areas and the proper disposal of trash. Although trash cans may be scarce, most Japanese citizens don't find this inconvenient. It's already an established practice to carry the wrappers of their snacks or the empty plastic bottles they've used in their bags until they reach a suitable disposal point, typically at home. This cultural ethos reinforces the collective commitment to cleanliness in public spaces.

TRADITIONAL EVENTS AND FESTIVALS WORTH EXPERIENCING

Hanami

We briefly touched on Hanami in Chapter 1; now it's time to cover how you can enjoy this delightful blossom-viewing event. It can be as simple as a leisurely stroll through a park, but it traditionally involves a joyous picnic celebration beneath the blooming trees. Hanami gatherings have been a cherished tradition in Japan for centuries and continue to be hosted in both public and private gardens and parks throughout the nation.

Observing proper Hanami etiquette is essential to ensure a harmonious experience:

- **Respect local regulations:** Familiarize yourself with and adhere to the specific rules of the park you are visiting, as these rules can vary. For instance, many parks prohibit barbecuing, a few may not allow alcoholic beverages, and some have evening curfews.
- **Dispose of garbage responsibly:** Remember the trash can section above. Be mindful of your trash and dispose of it appropriately. This may mean that you'll need to carry your garbage back home with you.

- **Handle the trees with care:** Avoid pulling, shaking, or picking the branches or blossoms, and refrain from climbing the trees or standing on their roots.

Gion Matsuri in Kyoto

Gion Matsuri, celebrated at Yasaka Shrine, stands as Japan's most renowned festival, spanning the entire month of July. Throughout this festive month, a myriad of events unfolds, with the highlight being the magnificent grand float procession known as Yamaboko Junko, held on July 17.

Interestingly, the most anticipated events of Gion Matsuri don't unfold in the Gion district itself but instead on the opposite bank of the Kamo River. In the days leading up to the grand procession, the respective yama and hoko floats are showcased within approximately half a kilometer of the Karasuma and Shijo intersection. During their display, some of these floats are open for exploration by tourists. The atmosphere truly comes alive in the evenings when streets are cordoned off from traffic, and the area teems with food stalls, beverage vendors, and other quintessential festival elements.

The float processions (Yamaboko Junko) occur on the 17th, following a three-kilometer route along Shijo, Kawaramachi, and Oike streets. While some paid seating options are available in front of the city hall, there are plenty of good vantage points along the route to enjoy the processions without much difficulty.

Tanabata Festival

Tanabata, also known as the "star festival," is observed on the 7th day of the 7th month of the year. This celebration stems from a Chinese legend in which the two stars, Altair and Vega, typically separated by the Milky Way, are said to reunite on this day. Interestingly, due to the alignment with the former lunar calendar, Tanabata is still marked on August 7 in certain regions of Japan, while in others, it occurs on July 7.

A cherished Tanabata tradition involves writing one's wishes on a piece of paper and hanging it on a specially prepared bamboo tree, hoping these wishes will come true. Vibrant Tanabata festivals are conducted throughout Japan in early July and August. Notable ones include the Sendai Tanabata festival in August and the Hiratsuka festival near Tokyo in July.

Obon Festival

Obon is a significant Japanese festival celebrated annually in either July or August, depending on the region. It's an annual Buddhist occasion deeply rooted in the practice of commemorating one's ancestors. During Obon, it is believed that the spirits of these departed ancestors return to the earthly realm to visit their living relatives.

Traditionally, households hang lanterns outside their homes to symbolically guide the spirits of their ancestors. Communities come alive with the rhythmic and graceful performances of obon dances, known as bon odori. Families pay respects to their ancestors by visiting their graves and offering food at home altars.

As Obon draws to a close, a beautiful and poignant ritual involves setting floating lanterns adrift in rivers, lakes, and seas, serving as luminous guides to lead the ancestral spirits back to their world. It's important to note that the customs and traditions associated with Obon can vary significantly from one region to another.

Winter Illuminations

Winter illuminations, a cherished tradition during the Christmas and New Year seasons, have gained immense popularity in cities throughout Japan. These enchanting light displays typically grace the urban landscapes from November to December. However, some extend their luminous presence even further, commencing as early as October and lingering until Valentine's Day or even the arrival of spring.

Among the pioneers of Japan's dazzling light spectacles is Kobe's Luminarie, a festival illuminated with Italian design. This remarkable event was created as a tribute to the victims of the devastating Kobe earthquake in 1995, making it one of the nation's earliest and most spectacular light shows.

THE PURPOSE OF MATSURI

The fundamental purpose of Japanese cultural festivals is rooted in expressing gratitude to the divine. The word "Matsuri" itself, with its etymological origins in "enshrined," encapsulates the essence of seeking solace, offering prayers, and showing appreciation for the intricate rhythms of nature. These festivals trace their roots back to indigenous beliefs encompassing Shamanism, Shintoism, and Buddhism. To grasp the sentiments associated with Japanese festivals, one must grasp the pivotal concepts of "Hare" and "Ke." "Hare" represents the extraordinary, a departure from the everyday "Ke" routine. Festivals embody the spirit of "Hare," serving as a splendid reset to the routine of "Ke."

Japanese individuals eagerly anticipate these moments of "Hare" as they infuse vitality into their daily "Ke" existence. Beyond their divine origins, festivals take on various forms, including those dedicated to regional rejuvenation. Seasonal festivals, such as the Cherry Blossom Festival and Snow Festival, are inspired by the changing seasons. Era-themed festivals and victory parades commemorate significant historical triumphs. Additionally, festivals with foreign origins, exemplified by events like the lively Spring Festival and Samba Carnival, have found a place within Japan's rich festival landscape.

TO SUMMARIZE

In this chapter, we had a look at the following topics:

- etiquette and cultural norms to be aware of
- traditional events and festivals worth experiencing
- the purpose of matsuri

As you journey through Japan, remember that a little understanding and respect for local customs can go a long way in enhancing your experience. So, put these insights into action and make every moment count. Coming up next, we're diving into Japan's diverse natural landscapes.

The Fascinating World of Sampuru

> *"Japanese culture is one of the very few cultures left that is its own entity. They're just so traditional and so specific in their ways. It's kind of untouched, it's not Americanized." – Toni Collette*

By the time you've visited a few restaurants in Japan, you'll be familiar with fake food. Outside many eating establishments, or displayed in the windows, you'll find replicas of the dishes on offer inside – much like an illustrated menu, only in three dimensions. Better yet, some of them are animated!

These sculptures, known as "sampuru" (akin to the English word, "sample") are handmade, generally out of PVC. What's most fascinating about them is that they're often made bespoke, which means that they match the style of the food you'll see inside.

If you find yourself fascinated by this phenomenon, visit Kitchen Street, formally known as Kappabashi Street. You'll find it between Asakusa and Ueno in Tokyo, and it's the place where restaurants order their sampuru. If you're a kitchen-lover, there are plenty of beautiful kitchen items to browse through too.

Restaurants that do this let customers know exactly what they can expect when they go inside, so it's a great way for you to decide on the perfect dinner spot. And while we've paused on this interesting fact, I'd like to invite you to do the same for this book. You don't have to create a replica of it, but you can let new readers know what they can expect by leaving your feedback online.

By leaving a review of this book on Amazon, you'll show other readers who are looking for a travel guide to help them plan their adventure to Japan exactly where they can find it.

Just as sampuru shows diners what they'll be served, your review will let new readers know what they can expect to find in this book.

Thank you so much for your support. You're helping fellow travelers all over the world!

Scan the QR code below to leave your review!

5

IMMERSING IN NATURE—JAPAN'S BREATHTAKING LANDSCAPES

While Japan is often recognized for its vibrant and bustling urban hubs, the country's geographical diversity extends far beyond its cities. In fact, Japan's landscape comprises over 70% mountainous terrain, offering a captivating tapestry of natural beauty that ranges from lush tropical environments to breathtaking icy peaks. This means that as you explore Japan, you'll have the opportunity to immerse yourself in an astonishing variety of landscapes, each with its own unique charm and character.

OVERVIEW: UNDERSTANDING THE GEOGRAPHICAL DIVERSITY OF JAPAN

Japan's unique geographical location in East Asia is a key factor that gifts the country with four distinct seasons, each characterized by its own natural beauty. Here's how Japan's position contributes to this phenomenon:

Proximity to the Asian Continent

Japan is situated relatively close to the Asian continent, which means it experiences a continental climate influence. During the winter months, cold air masses from Siberia sweep across the Sea of Japan, bringing frigid temperatures and heavy snowfall to certain regions. This results in Japan's picturesque winter landscapes, making it a popular destination for winter sports enthusiasts.

Pacific Ocean Influence

To the east of Japan lies the Pacific Ocean, which has a moderating effect on the climate. This oceanic influence is most prominent during the summer when Japan experiences the rainy season, known as "tsuyu" or the plum rain season. The warm, moist air from the Pacific Ocean brings ample rainfall, nourishing Japan's lush greenery and vibrant flora during this season.

Seasonal Shifts

Japan's unique position allows for clear seasonal shifts, with distinct temperature and weather pattern changes. Spring brings the famous cherry blossoms that blanket the country in delicate pink and white petals. Summers are characterized by warm and humid weather, making it an ideal time for outdoor festivals and enjoying the beaches. Autumn ushers in vibrant foliage, with leaves turning shades of red, orange, and yellow, creating stunning landscapes. Finally, winter transforms Japan's northern regions into a snowy wonderland, perfect for winter sports and hot spring (onsen) retreats.

Varied Geography

Japan's diverse topography, which includes mountains, forests, coastlines, and plains, further enhances the distinctiveness of its seasons. Different regions experience the seasons differently, with the timing of cherry blossom blooms, summer festivals, and fall foliage varying across the country. This geographical diversity ensures that travelers can enjoy Japan's natural beauty year-round, regardless of the season.

MOUNTAINS AND HIKING TRAILS

Mount Fuji

Mount Fuji, standing an impressive 12388 feet tall, proudly claims the title of Japan's tallest mountain. Its near-perfect conical shape has earned it geological significance and deep spiritual reverence. Over the centuries, this sacred volcano has captivated people's hearts from all walks of life.

As an active volcano, Mount Fuji last erupted in 1707, adding an element of dynamism to its otherwise serene presence. Located on the boundary between Yamanashi and Shizuoka prefectures, the majestic mountain often graces the skyline of Tokyo and Yokohama on clear days.

Another way to get a glimpse of Mount Fuji is on the train ride between Tokyo and Osaka. Riding the shinkansen from Tokyo toward Nagoya, Kyoto, and Osaka, one can enjoy the best view of the mountain from the right-hand side of the train around Shin-Fuji Station.

However, Mount Fuji's visibility is often subject to the capricious whims of clouds and weather conditions. A clear view of the mountain is indeed a fortunate sight. Generally, visibility tends to be clearer during the colder seasons of the year compared to the summer months. It is often more favorable in the early morning or late evening hours. For those seeking a more leisurely and immersive experience, the Fuji Five Lake (Fujigoko) region at the mountain's northern base and the nearby hot spring resort of Hakone provide picturesque natural settings in which to admire Mount Fuji's grandeur.

If the idea of conquering this iconic peak beckons to you, Mount Fuji welcomes hikers during its climbing season, which typically spans from early July to early September, with the peak season occurring between late July and late

August. The trails tend to be considerably busier around the Obon holidays, which occur during mid-August. Additionally, be aware that adverse weather conditions, such as rain or strong winds, may lead to trail closures. Therefore, it's crucial to plan your ascent with care.

Many climbers choose a two-day itinerary, which involves resting at a mountain hut located halfway up the peak before embarking on the final ascent to the summit in the early morning hours. This strategy allows you to reach the summit just in time to witness the breathtaking sunrise.

Japanese Alps

Over a century ago, during Japan's Meiji era, a British gentleman bestowed the name "The Japan Alps" upon the country's mountain ranges. While these peaks may not rival the towering heights of the Himalayas or the European Alps, they offer a unique appeal for enthusiasts who seek to explore elevations above 9,843 feet. Unlike icy summits that demand advanced climbing skills, Japan's mountains provide opportunities for climbing and captivating vistas that can stand proudly alongside their renowned counterparts.

This mountainous region boasts an array of diverse and enjoyable routes, catering to a wide range of preferences and extending over six prefectures, organized into the Southern, Central, and Northern regions. This vast expanse offers many hiking trails and tracks for hiking, accompanied by numerous temples, shrines, and historic post towns.

Nagano prefecture serves as the primary host to the Japan Alps, offering the broadest range of experiences for avid trekkers. The Hida Mountains boast some of Japan's most cherished hiking routes in the northern section. Heading southward, you'll encounter the somewhat milder Akaishi Mountains, and further beyond, picturesque rivers and lakes unfold, enhancing the region's allure.

Whether you're an experienced climber, a long-distance trail enthusiast, a forest hiking aficionado, or simply seeking to trek through plateaus to savor mountain panoramas, the Japanese Alps have something to offer. Additionally, during the winter months, numerous ski resorts in this region come to life, benefiting from the abundant snowfall that graces the area.

Today, the Japanese Alps have garnered the attention of climbers, mountain enthusiasts, skiers, and outdoor lovers from around the globe. They come in search of unique ways to embrace the distinct beauty and allure of Japan's mountains, reaffirming their status as a captivating destination for those passionate about the great outdoors.

Kumano Kodo

Kumano Kodo, also known as Kumano Kodō, is an extensive network of pilgrimage routes in Japan's southern

Kansai region. Pilgrims have traversed them. These ancient pathways, referred to as Kodo or "old ways," hold significant cultural and historical importance, playing a pivotal role in the region's designation as a UNESCO World Heritage site. Pilgrims have traversed them for over a millennium, making them a testament to Japan's rich spiritual heritage. Notably, Kumano Kodo shares the distinction of being recognized as a World Heritage site alongside the Camino de Santiago, highlighting its global significance.

The origins of these pilgrimage routes lie in their function as passages connecting sacred sites on the Kii Peninsula. The three renowned Kumano shrines are central to this religious landscape: Nachi Taisha, Hayatama Taisha, and Hongu Taisha, known together as Kumano Sanzan. By the 12th century, these shrines had gained widespread fame, attracting pilgrims from major cities like Kyoto and Osaka, as well as regions beyond. However, the significance of Kumano Kodo extends beyond mere transportation to these revered shrines; the trails themselves were designed to provide a profound spiritual experience. They often meander through challenging and occasionally treacherous mountain terrain, serving as a journey of devotion and self-discovery.

While many of the coastal trails have succumbed to modern development, several mountain trails and passes have endured, allowing modern-day pilgrims to trace the steps of their predecessors and experience the spiritual significance of Kumano Kodo. A typical journey along the historic Kumano Kodo trail spans approximately five days, yet shorter day treks without overnight stays are also available. While it's entirely feasible to walk the trails independently, there are numerous tour operators offering guided expeditions, streamlining the planning process and ensuring a more convenient and enriching hiking experience. These paths remain accessible throughout the year; however, weekends and holidays see increased foot traffic. Even on these bustling days, it's advisable to join fellow travelers to partake in one of Asia's most spiritually rewarding hikes.

ONSEN RESORTS

Japan enjoys a global reputation for its diverse range of incredible onsen and hot springs. Many travelers come to Japan with the sole purpose of visiting the onsen towns, while others find themselves irresistibly drawn to the enchantment of Japanese onsen, making return trips for revitalizing getaways. In the upcoming sections, I'll be unveiling six hot spring towns, each with its own distinctive allure.

Kusatsu Onsen, Gunma

Kusatsu is considered one of Japan's top three famous hot spring towns, attracting visitors from all corners of the country. What makes Kusatsu truly unique is its exceptional sulfuric waters, celebrated for their remarkable therapeutic qualities.

At the heart of this picturesque town lies the traditional Yubatake hot water field, where piping hot spring water surges to the surface and is then cooled before flowing into a variety of baths. The captivating spectacle of steam rising from the Yubatake serves as a testament to Kusatsu's deep cultural roots and the curative virtues of its hot springs.

A 15-minute walk from the Yubatake will lead you to the timeless Sainokawara Open-Air Bath. This expansive outdoor onsen invites you to relish the ever-changing seasons while immersing yourself in a soothing soak. It's even available in the evenings, offering a tranquil environment to unwind in the curative waters beneath a canopy of stars. On Fridays, the men's bath welcomes mixed bathing, allowing guests in swimsuits to partake in the hot springs together. If you're spending the night in Kusatsu Onsen town, make sure not to overlook the enchanting nighttime spectacle of the Yubatake. As the lights dance on the spring waters and mist weaves through the air, it conjures a captivating and almost otherworldly ambiance.

Kinosaki Onsen, Hyogo

If you seek the ambiance of a traditional Japanese city, then Kinosaki is the ideal destination. Nestled in the picturesque Hyogo region, this charming onsen town is renowned for its traditional character and quaint allure. Graceful willow trees line its streets, cultivating a serene atmosphere.

The origins of Kinosaki can be traced back to the year 720 when Mandara-Yu, its earliest hot spring, marked the town's birth. The chronicles recount the journey of a compassionate priest who embarked on a quest to aid those in need. His voyage eventually brought him to Kinosaki Onsen, where, according to local legend, an oracle instructed him to undertake 1,000 days of prayer to alleviate the people's suffering. Astonishingly, upon completing this monumental undertaking, a hot spring miraculously surged forth. Revered for its exceptional curative properties, this spring quickly gained fame throughout the region and far beyond.

The name "Mandara," evoking an enlightened mind, embodies the onsen's spiritual heritage. In the modern era, Kinosaki pays homage to its legacy through seven public bathhouses, each exuding a unique atmosphere and therapeutic offerings, with the venerable Mandara-Yu continuing to welcome visitors, much as it has for centuries.

To fully embrace the local customs, visitors can wear a yukata, a lightweight cotton kimono, and meander through the town, moving from one bathhouse to another. This delightful practice offers an authentic and soothing experience, enabling travelers to unwind and absorb the rich traditions of Kinosaki Onsen.

Beppu Onsen, Oita

Beppu is situated on the scenic southern island of Kyushu, known for its abundant hot spring sources, boasting the highest volume of gushing water and the greatest number of hot spring sources. Beppu City is home to eight distinct hot spring resorts collectively known as the "Beppu Hatto." Each of these resorts possesses unique characteristics, including variations in spring quality, offering the opportunity to embark on a captivating "hot spring tour" right within Beppu City.

A must-see attraction for sightseeing in Beppu is the Beppu Jigoku Tour, which features the famous "hells" (jigoku) of Beppu. These seven extraordinary hot springs are meant for viewing rather than bathing and showcase steaming ponds of various colors and bubbling mud pools. Among them, the Chinoike Jigoku, or "blood pond hell," stands out with its striking hot red water and a sizable souvenir shop.

Where bathing options are concerned, Beppu provides a diverse range, including traditional hot spring baths. However, what truly distinguishes it are the exceptional sand and mud baths. These extraordinary natural phenomena allow visitors to immerse themselves in warm, therapeutic sands or indulge in mineral-rich mud, believed to possess therapeutic qualities.

Nozawa Onsen and Shibu Onsen, Nagano

Are you a winter enthusiast or a ski aficionado? Then, make sure to stop by Nozawa Onsen, also known as Nozawa Onsen Snow Resort. Nozawa is one of the most renowned onsen retreats in the Chubu region of Honshu. It's not only celebrated for its therapeutic hot springs but also for its well-loved ski resort. This fame reached an international level when it served as one of the venues for the 1998 Nagano Olympics.

At the foot of Mt. Kenashi lies the picturesque town of Nozawa Onsen, where you'll find thirteen distinctive public bathhouses collectively known as "SOTOYU." Visitors are encouraged to take part in a soothing onsen pilgrimage by exploring these bathhouses.

Be sure not to overlook Ogama, the town's communal open-air kitchen and home to the hottest of Nozawa Onsen's thirty natural spring sources. The locals make use of Ogama's five pools of steaming-hot mineral water, reaching temperatures of 194 °F, for various purposes, including washing, soaking vines for weaving, and cooking vegetables and eggs. The mineral-rich water imparts a unique flavor to the food, especially the region's signature leafy green, Nozawa-na.

For those not inclined towards skiing, the nearby Shibu Onsen provides an excellent alternative for indulging in a hot spring bath. This onsen town, boasting a history spanning over 1300 years, exudes a historical charm with its cobblestone streets and traditional ryokan inns, offering a glimpse into the past.

Both Nozawa Onsen and Shibu Onsen also offer convenient access to the Jigokudani Monkey Park. In this enchanting winter wonderland, you can witness snow monkeys playing and bathing in natural hot springs, a heartwarming spectacle that has captivated millions around the world. Spend your days experiencing the thrill of skiing at Nozawa Onsen Ski Resort or observing the adorable snow monkeys, and let your evenings unwind as the hot springs rejuvenate your body and soul. Remarkably, both Nozawa Onsen and Shibu Onsen are enchanting destinations worth visiting throughout the year.

Dogo Onsen, Ehime

If you're a fan of Ghibli films, you may have wondered about the real-life inspiration for Yubaba's "Aburaya," the iconic bathhouse where Japanese and Western architectural styles blend into the beloved Ghibli film *Spirited Away*. It's believed that the model for this enchanting bathhouse is none other than the Dogo Onsen Honkan in Dogo Onsen town.

Dogo is known for being one of Japan's oldest and historically significant onsen towns, with a legacy that spans centuries, providing a captivating glimpse into Japan's cultural heritage. The Dogo Onsen Honkan, majestically positioned at the heart of the onsen town and surrounded by natural hot springs, boasts elegant architecture and a treasure trove of tradition. Additionally, a new, vibrant shopping district awaits your exploration.

One distinguishing feature of Dogo Onsen is its direct use of hot spring water from the source, without the need for reheating or additional water. The town is home to 18 natural hot spring sources, each offering water at temperatures ranging from 68 to 131 °F. This pumped water is collected in what's known as a hot spring supply facility, where water of varying temperatures is blended and adjusted to maintain a constant temperature before being distributed to public bathhouses.

Beyond the serene onsen experience, there are numerous attractions for you to discover. One popular site is the Sora-no-Sanpomichi, an observation promenade situated atop Mt. Kanmuriyama on the southern side of Dogo Onsen Honkan. It presents a breathtaking view of Dogo Onsen Honkan below and the expanse of the Dogo town. This observation point is thoughtfully equipped with arbors and benches, and it even features a footbath with hot spring water directly from the source, allowing you to savor the scenery while indulging in a soothing soak.

NATIONAL PARKS AND PROTECTED AREAS

Shiretoko National Park

Shiretoko National Park, situated in eastern Hokkaido's Shiretoko Peninsula, stands out as one of Japan's most exquisite and untouched national parks. The peninsula is characterized by its inherent isolation, with roads extending only about three-quarters of the way up the peninsula. As for the northernmost tip, it can only be observed from boats or accessed through extended hiking excursions spanning multiple days.

Within this pristine natural environment, an array of wildlife thrives, including deer, foxes, and brown bears. During winter, the coastal region along the Sea of Okhotsk becomes one of the best places in Japan to witness the stunning phenomenon of drift ice. Shiretoko was inscribed as a UNESCO World Heritage site in 2005 to recognize the peninsula's invaluable ecosystem and biodiversity.

Ogasawara Islands

The Ogasawara Islands, also known as the Bonin Islands, constitute a string of volcanic islands situated in the Pacific Ocean. They are positioned approximately 621 miles to the south and are under the administrative jurisdiction of Tokyo. Access to these islands is limited to a weekly ferry service from Tokyo, which entails a 24-hour journey. Of all the islands in this chain, only Chichijima, often referred to as "Father Island," and Hahajima, known as "Mother Island," are inhabited.

Sharing a similar geographical latitude with Okinawa, the Ogasawara Islands enjoy a subtropical climate marked by consistently warm temperatures throughout the year. These islands entice visitors with their secluded ambiance, warm hospitality, pristine beaches, vibrant coral reefs, and lush jungles covering their hills. Moreover, they offer a range of outdoor activities such as hiking, diving, snorkeling, sea kayaking, swimming with dolphins, and whale watching.

Because the Ogasawara Islands have remained isolated from the Japanese mainland and other continents, they harbor a wealth of unique plant and animal species found nowhere else. These include crabs, insects, and birds that have adapted exclusively to this environment. Therefore, camping and off-trail hiking are strictly prohibited across the island chain to prevent any harm to the local fauna and flora.

Aso-Kuju National Park

Serving as a central attraction in Kyushu, the Aso-Kuju National Park is aptly named for its focal points, the active volcanoes of Mount Aso and the Kuju Mountains. Additionally, it encompasses Mount Yufu, offering commanding views of Yufuin Onsen, and Mount Tsurumi, located above Beppu. Established in 1934, the Aso-Kuju National Park holds the distinction of being one of Japan's oldest national parks.

Within the confines of this national park lies an unparalleled opportunity to explore dramatic volcanic terrains and witness the majesty of active volcanoes. Mount Aso invites tourists to catch a glimpse of its active crater, while the Kuju Mountains, which rank as the highest peaks on Kyushu Island, beckon hikers with a well-designed network of trails. Naturally, these volcanoes give rise to the emergence of hot springs, providing sustenance for some of Japan's most celebrated onsen towns, including Beppu, Yufuin, and Kurokawa.

Daisetsuzan National Park

Daisetsuzan National Park, situated in Hokkaido Prefecture, takes the title of Japan's most mountainous and largest national park among the 34 in the country. Encompassing a sprawling area of approximately 876 square miles, it boasts a diverse range of plant and animal species, some of which are exceedingly rare. Within the volcanic expanse of the Daisetsuzan group, you'll find Mount Asahidake, the highest peak in Hokkaido at 7516 feet, alongside several other active volcanoes.

While snow and ice dominate the landscape for much of the year, the short summer season unveils a vivid tapestry of alpine flora, blanketing the expansive, treeless plateaus of the alpine zone. Known as Kamui Mintara, or "playground of the gods," to Hokkaido's indigenous Ainu people, Daisetsuzan is a realm where nature's grandeur reigns supreme.

TO SUMMARIZE

In this chapter, we explored the following topics:

- the geographical diversity of Japan
- mountains and hiking trails
- onsen resorts
- national parks and protected areas

Having immersed ourselves in the natural landscapes of Japan, it's time to satiate our appetites. As we step into the bustling streets of Tokyo or the tranquil by-lanes of Kyoto, the aroma of Japan's culinary delights beckons. In the next chapter, we embark on a gastronomic journey, exploring the iconic dishes of Japan and the stories behind them. Prepare your taste buds for "Gastronomic Adventures!"

6

GASTRONOMIC ADVENTURES

There is no better way to experience Japan than through its food, a culinary adventure that tantalizes the senses and captures the essence of the country's rich culture. Japanese cuisine is globally recognized for its distinctive, wholesome, fresh, and delectable ingredients and its remarkable culinary presentation. Traditional Japanese food is one of the world's most cherished and widely embraced cuisines, to the extent that it has earned a place on UNESCO's "Intangible Cultural Heritage" list. This widespread acclaim is reflected in Tokyo, Japan's capital, which boasts the world's largest number of restaurants, including the most Michelin-starred establishments.

ICONIC JAPANESE DISHES AND THEIR SIGNIFICANCE

Sushi: A Regional Delight

Japan is widely recognized as the sushi hub of the world, where this iconic dish was first introduced to global travelers. However, sushi's roots can be traced back to a Chinese culinary creation known as narezushi. This early version of sushi featured fermented rice and salted fish, with the surprising fact that it wasn't prepared for flavor. The origins of this dish can be traced as far back as the 2nd century BC, a staggering 2,000 years before the invention of refrigerators.

Since then, sushi has undergone numerous international reinventions and, interestingly, has also evolved distinctively within Japan over the centuries. Various regions within Japan have cultivated their unique interpretations of sushi, preserving a rich diversity of styles. Let's look at two of them, with the former redefining the traditional concept of sushi and the latter distinguishing itself with its unique presentation and packaging.

Kansai's Mushi Sushi

Sushi doesn't always require raw ingredients, nor is it always served at body temperature or cold. This diversity is wonderfully exemplified by mushi sushi. This type of sushi involves arranging various cooked ingredients on seasoned rice and then gently steaming the entire combination. This preparation aligns with chirashi sushi, which features a bowl of rice topped with finely chopped ingredients. The name "mushi sushi" is derived from the method of preparation, as the Japanese word "mushi" means "to steam."

Nara's Kakinoha Sushi

Kakinoha sushi, literally translating to "sushi with persimmon leaf," is a culinary delight that hails from Nara. It comprises bite-sized portions of vinegared rice and sashimi, typically salmon or mackerel, snugly wrapped in "kakinoha," or persimmon leaves, and elegantly arranged in a wooden box.

Nara's inland location made seafood transportation challenging during the Edo era. Therefore, persimmon leaf was ingeniously used to wrap the sushi and preserve its flavor. In addition to its preservative function, the leaf possesses natural antibacterial properties.

While the persimmon leaf itself isn't edible, it imparts a delicate, slightly sweet aroma to the sushi. For a harmonious flavor combination, consider the mackerel kakinoha sushi, as the fish readily absorbs the subtle aroma of the persimmon leaf.

Ramen: The Ultimate Comfort Food

In 1910, a Chinese restaurant located in Tokyo's Asakusa district introduced a ramen dish to its patrons. This dish featured Chinese-style wheat noodles immersed in a flavorful meat- or fish-based broth, quickly captivating the public's taste buds. Although Japanese cuisine already included popular noodle options like soba and udon, incorporating kansui, an alkaline solution, imparted the distinctive springy texture that ramen noodles are known for.

Fast forward to August 1945, amid the devastation of war-torn Osaka, a man named Momofuku Ando stumbled upon a peculiar sight—a makeshift ramen stand set up amidst the debris, where people patiently waited for a bowl of this comforting dish. The image left an indelible mark on the businessman. Thirteen years later, he would refine his recipe for instant ramen and unveil it to the world. Now, ramen is more than just a bowl of wheat noodles, a flavorful broth, and toppings. It's also a convenient and universally loved delight transcending its Japanese origins.

The heart and soul of ramen reside within its broth, which falls into five primary categories: Miso, Tori Paitan, Tonkotsu, Shio, and Shoyu.

Miso ramen's broth texture is what sets it apart from the rest. Originating from Hokkaido, it boasts a unique flavor achieved by stir-frying miso with vegetables and broth in a Chinese wok. A lard topping adds an extra dimension to the taste while aiding in maintaining the soup's warmth.

Tori Paitan and Tonkotsu form an intriguing pair, both characterized by their cloudy, velvety broths. Tonkotsu stands out with its sumptuously thick broth, a result of the protracted simmering of pork bones, resulting in a profoundly pork-flavored soup. Meanwhile, Tori Paitan's opaqueness emerges from the extended cooking of chicken, imparting a unique profile distinct from its pork-based counterpart.

Shio ramen embodies a delicate, clear essence. Its name, "Shio," literally means "salt" in Japanese. Though the broth is typically made with chicken, seafood and pork renditions exist.

Lastly, we have Shoyu ramen, which is beloved throughout Japan. It marries a blend of soy sauce and dashi (broth), which may encompass pork, chicken, or seafood, with variations depending on the region and eatery.

Tempura: The Art of Deep-Frying

Tempura is a beloved Japanese delicacy featuring meats, seafood, and vegetables deep-fried to golden perfection in a delicate batter. A soy-based dipping sauce customarily accompanies this delectable dish and is commonly relished as either a flavorful appetizer or a satisfying, light meal. With its rich history spanning centuries and a delightful taste that appeals to palates worldwide, tempura has earned its global popularity.

Tempura's origins trace back to the 16th century when it is believed to have been introduced to Japan by Portuguese missionaries and traders who shared their deep-frying culinary technique. The Japanese adapted this cooking method to their own cuisine by incorporating local ingredients.

The term "tempura" finds its roots in the Latin word "tempora," meaning "seasonal." This name reflects the practice of preparing tempura as a seasonal delicacy, with ingredients being deep-fried only during specific times of the year when they were in abundance. It also served as a means of preserving food, allowing it to stay fresh and maintain its flavor.

With the passage of time, tempura steadily gained popularity until it became a fundamental component of the Japanese diet. Its appeal has also extended thanks to its adaptability. It's a straightforward dish to make and can be relished with an array of ingredients. Tempura can also be incorporated into soups, salads, and various other recipes. Additionally, it's a sought-after ingredient for sushi rolls, adding a delightful crunch and flavor to this beloved Japanese delicacy.

Okonomiyaki: Japan's Savory Pancakes

Okonomiyaki is often thought of as a Japanese pizza or savory pancake. Its batter typically features eggs, flour, cabbage, tempura scraps (tenkasu), and pork belly slices. What makes it truly special are the various toppings and condiments, including Japanese mayonnaise, okonomiyaki sauce, dried bonito flakes, and dried seaweed.

The roots of okonomiyaki can be traced back to Sen no Rikyu, a tea ceremony master renowned for his role in the history of Matcha. As the legend goes, during one of his tea ceremonies, Sen no Rikyu served a cake known as "fu-no yaki." This cake was crafted by mixing flour with water and then roasting this blend before thinly spreading it on a pot to cook.

In Osaka, before World War II, a local snack called "yoshokuyaki" started to gain popularity. This snack initially consisted of a simple mixture of flour and water spread on a griddle with cabbage on top, primarily enjoyed by children. However, as green onions, pork, and seafood made their way into the dish, adults wanted some, too. The name "okonomiyaki" was eventually bestowed upon this evolving culinary creation, signifying its adaptability to various preferred (konomi) ingredients.

After World War II, okonomiyaki restaurants, influenced by prevailing poverty and food shortages, began offering dishes made from affordable ingredients. These eateries quickly expanded beyond Osaka, spanning the entire Kansai region. After being featured on television during the 1970s, okonomiyaki restaurants garnered nationwide attention.

Okonomiyaki primarily comes in two major styles: Hiroshima-style and Kansai-style. The difference lies in their preparation methods. Hiroshima-style okonomiyaki layers the batter and ingredients separately on the griddle, often incorporating noodles. In contrast, Kansai-style okonomiyaki involves mixing the ingredients with the batter before cooking.

A closely related variant to okonomiyaki is "monjayaki." This beloved Tokyo dish features a thinner batter seasoned with sauce or shoyu before cooking. Nowadays, specialty restaurants offer monjayaki, and many of them also include okonomiyaki on their menus.

Matcha: The Heart of the Tea Ceremony

Matcha, the vibrant green tea that's finely ground into a powder, holds a rich history in Japan, shaped by remarkable individuals who left an enduring legacy. In the 9th century, revered Buddhist scholars Saicho and Kukai journeyed to China. Their travels not only brought back wisdom but also the very first tea seeds to Japanese soil.

Then, in the year 1187, a Tendai monk named Myoan Eisai, went to China as well, where he also stumbled upon the tea seeds in addition to Zen scriptures. As the 15th century dawned, matcha's fate was inextricably tied to Zen Buddhism, giving rise to "sado" or the Way of Tea, more commonly known as the tea ceremony.

But the real luminary of sado was Sen no Rikyu. From an early age, he delved into the profound teachings of both tea and Zen. In 1579, he took up the mantle of tea master for the renowned samurai Oda Nobunaga. Even after Nobunaga's passing, Sen no Rikyu's influence remained strong as he continued to shape the essence and cultural significance of matcha in Japan.

For a while, the tea ceremony was a realm reserved for the upper echelons of society, the exclusive gatekeeper to the world of matcha. Yet, a shift occurred, driven by advancements in production and processing, resulting in green tea powder gradually finding its way into the hands of the wider Japanese public. It no longer remained an elitist delight but became an accessible treasure enjoyed on various occasions, whether it's a laid-back gathering or a formal affair.

In today's Japan, matcha has transcended its status as a mere beverage. It's transformed into a versatile ingredient treasured for its vivid green hue and unparalleled flavor. From sweet to savory, matcha weaves its enchantment, introducing a spectrum of tastes and textures to culinary creations.

Uji, the Renowned Matcha Town

When you're planning your journey through Japan and find yourself in Kyoto and Osaka, there's an experience that's not to be missed. Just a short 20- to 30-minute ride from Kyoto on the JR Nara Line, Uji beckons you into the epicenter of Japanese tea culture, the town of matcha. Here, you can fully immerse yourself in the authentic world of Matcha cuisine and explore the highest quality matcha and green tea.

Here, you'll find the Nakamura Tokichi Honten, a beloved café that has its roots as a tea factory dating back to the Meiji period. Following a tasteful renovation in 2001, this establishment has risen to great acclaim. Here, you're offered a wonderful choice: participate in a full-fledged tea ceremony (reservation required) or indulge in an array of matcha-inspired dishes, spanning from savory soba noodles to heavenly desserts.

Among the café's most exquisite offerings is the tea jelly set, a delightful ensemble featuring matcha-infused ice cream, sweet red beans, chewy mochi balls, and matcha jelly presented in bamboo bowls. Additionally, you'll be presented with a palette of green tea drinks to choose from. What makes this dining experience even more exceptional is the café's beautifully designed Japanese garden, adorned with centuries-old trees that form a captivating view while you enjoy your meal.

Considering Nakamura Tokichi Honten's popularity among both locals and tourists, it's advisable to prepare for a wait of approximately 40 to 90 minutes before you're comfortably seated. While you're waiting, make the most of your time by browsing through the shop's tea-related souvenirs. Alternatively, you can walk along Byodo-In Omotesando Street, a charming lane lined with shops specializing in tea and tea-related products. If you're eager to explore the world of matcha cuisine without the wait, this picturesque street offers an array of authentic matcha-flavored delights. Satisfy your taste buds with treats like matcha dango (Japanese dumplings), matcha parfait, and matcha Zenzai, a sweet red bean soup.

While you're in Uji, consider a visit to the unique Uji Starbucks, a rare gem among Starbucks locations in Japan, offering the enchanting view of a Japanese garden. This particular branch is conveniently located on the way to the World Heritage site, Byodo-In Temple. If you fancy a change of pace from matcha, I suggest a stroll along the Uji River. Make your way across the Uji Bridge, which spans the Uji River and is renowned as one of Japan's three iconic old bridges. This short journey will immerse you in the distinctive atmosphere of Uji, allowing you to savor the moments in a truly special setting.

Seafood: Treasures of Japan's Coastal Cuisine

Japan's abundant coastline, enveloped by the bountiful sea, grants it extensive access to seafood delights and an array of marine offerings. To truly submerge yourself in the world of Japanese seafood, there's no better way than by exploring the local fish markets. These markets are not just about seafood; they're vibrant hubs where you can also discover fruit stalls, flower shops, restaurants, and much more. Let's explore two of Japan's renowned fish markets, one in the eastern region (Kanto) and the other in the western region (Kansai).

Tsukiji Outer Market, Tokyo, Kanto

Once known as the Tsukiji Wholesale Market, this bustling hub encompassed both inner and outer markets. The inner market, steeped in history since the 16th century, was the epicenter for wholesale transactions and home to the renowned morning tuna auctions. However, as preparations for the 2018 Tokyo Olympics got underway, the inner market relocated to Toyosu, emerging as the Toyosu Fish Market. Meanwhile, Tsukiji Outer Market continued to flourish, with a vibrant mix of wholesalers, shops, and delightful dining establishments.

At Tsukiji Outer Market, sushi undoubtedly reigns supreme, and the standout seafood delight is the Kaisendon. This delicious dish features a bowl of rice adorned with a tantalizing assortment of fresh raw seafood, known as sashimi. What distinguishes the Kaisendon at Tsukiji Outer Market is its unparalleled freshness and pleasant sweetness. The market's commitment to freshness is unwavering, as a substantial portion of the seafood served and available for purchase is sourced directly from the Toyosu Market, solidifying Tsukiji Outer Market's status as one of Tokyo's top destinations for savoring the freshest seafood. Tsukiji Outer Market kicks off early, with restaurants welcoming guests at 5 a.m. to cater to early risers and serving delectable seafood until early afternoon, around 2 p.m.

Kuromon Ichiba Market, Osaka, Kansai

Kuromon Ichiba Market, often affectionately referred to as "Osaka's kitchen," is truly the epicenter of the city's culinary scene. Stretching across approximately 150 vibrant stalls, this market is a gastronomic treasure trove, strongly emphasizing offering the freshest produce, meats, and especially seafood, which takes up a quarter of Kuromon Ichiba's stalls. You'll find everything from salmon, prawns, crab, pufferfish, oysters, and sea urchins.

While exploring this market, you'll have the chance to partake in Osaka's Tabe Aruki culture, a tradition that lets you savor your discoveries while strolling through the lively aisles. Beyond seafood, Kuromon Ichiba spoils you with an enticing selection of fresh fruits, vegetables, and premium wagyu beef, offering a haven for food enthusiasts in search of an authentic taste of Osaka.

RECOMMENDED PLACES TO EAT

Conveyor Belt Sushi Restaurants

Kaiten-sushi is a fast-food sushi style that originated in Japan, characterized by plates of sushi rotating around the restaurant on a conveyor belt. In Japanese, it's known as "kaiten-zushi," which translates to "rotating sushi." This differs from the traditional sushi dining experience, where customers typically sit at the counter and directly order their sushi from the staff. The concept of kaiten-sushi was initially devised to help sushi restaurants efficiently serve a larger number of customers with fewer servers. Beyond Japan, kaiten-sushi is occasionally referred to as "sushi boats" or "sushi trains" because some establishments present their sushi on small floating boats or miniature train carriages in addition to the traditional conveyor belt.

Yatai

Yatai are charming small open-air mobile food stands and a common sight at Matsuri or outside Shinto shrines during cultural celebrations. During Matsuri, these yatai offer a delightful array of freshly prepared Japanese street foods, including favorites like yakisoba (stir-fried noodles), takoyaki (crispy octopus-filled balls), and chocolate-dipped bananas.

Although yatai once held a prominent place in Japanese culture, they are now primarily associated with Matsuri events. However, in Fukuoka, a vibrant city situated in Kyushu, the southernmost of Japan's four major islands, the yatai tradition remains alive and thriving. Here, you'll discover over 100 yatai, providing a captivating glimpse into the city's nightlife. These mobile stalls start setting up around 6 p.m. each evening, transforming the cityscape into a haven of culinary delights. The classic yatai offerings encompass mouthwatering treats like tempura, ramen, oden (a one-pot dish brimming with assorted ingredients in a light, soy-infused dashi broth), and yakitori (grilled chicken).

However, you'll also encounter modern yatai that take fusion cuisine to the next level with dishes like Western-inspired Japanese creations and beef tongue. To complement these delectable bites, the beverage menu is equally enticing, featuring a selection of beers, shochu, and sake.

Although most yatai are compact, typically accommodating around 8 to 10 patrons, their cozy size creates a relaxed and intimate atmosphere. It's effortless to strike up conversations with fellow diners and perhaps make new friends while savoring the flavors of Fukuoka's yatai scene.

Traditional Izakaya

Izakaya are laid-back drinking establishments reminiscent of tapas bars, where patrons can order an array of small, shareable dishes. They are among the most prevalent types of restaurants in Japan, making them a favored choice for gatherings with friends or colleagues, whether it's a lively drinking session or a post-work relaxation spot. For tourists, izakaya presents an excellent dining option, as they are conveniently situated near train stations and entertainment districts, ranging from cozy single-counter joints to multi-story chain venues.

The izakaya menu often boasts a diverse selection of Japanese and occasionally international dishes. Typical offerings include yakitori, sashimi, grilled meats and seafood, regional specialties, fried delicacies, salads, hot pot creations, and noodle and rice dishes.

As establishments primarily centered around drinks, izakaya also features an extensive beverage selection, encompassing domestic and occasionally imported options like beer, sake, and shochu. Most menu items are priced at a few hundred yen each, resulting in an average meal cost ranging from ¥2,000–¥5,000 (around $13.40–$33.45) per person. Some izakaya even provide all-you-can-drink packages, typically starting at around ¥2,000 for a 90- to 120-minute duration.

High-End Kaiseki Restaurants

Kaiseki is a traditional Japanese multi-course dining experience typically offered at upscale Japanese restaurants. This culinary tradition features a meticulously curated sequence of small, artfully prepared dishes, each thoughtfully composed and presented to create a harmonious and memorable meal.

The kaiseki meal begins with "Sakizuke," which serves as an appetizer, followed by "Mukozuke," featuring delicate slices of raw fish, often presented as sashimi. This progression of courses continues, each dish showcasing seasonal ingredients, simple yet precise seasoning, and an artful presentation.

Kaiseki's roots trace back to its role as a special meal served before traditional tea ceremonies. In this context, the tea ceremony host prepared kaiseki to welcome guests warmly. This historical connection to hospitality is retained in modern kaiseki, where the emphasis remains on three key elements: seasonal ingredients, minimal seasoning to accentuate natural flavors and meticulous presentation. The result embodies wabi-sabi, an aesthetic philosophy that finds beauty in simplicity and imperfection, right on your dining table.

Themed Cafes

Themed cafes are dining establishments that are designed around a particular theme, concept, or idea. These themes can range from pop culture and fictional worlds to animals, hobbies, and more.

One of the most distinctive cafe categories you'll find in Japan is the animal-themed cafe. These charming cafes offer more than just a meal; they give visitors a unique opportunity to interact with and cuddle with adorable animals, creating a delightful and soothing atmosphere. It's a chance to make heartwarming memories with these fluffy companions. You can choose from a variety of options, including dog, cat, rabbit, and even owl cafes.

Anime-theme cafes are also wildly popular and well worth the visit. Some of the most notable ones include Shirohige's Cream Puff Factory (inspired by Studio Ghibli), the Pokemon Café, and Animate Cafe. The latter is a collaborative concept cafe that regularly updates its themes to feature different popular anime series. While Shirohige's Cream Puff Factory and the Pokemon Café are situated in Tokyo, Animate Cafe has branches throughout Japan and even abroad. Please note that reservations are essential for these cafes.

TO SUMMARIZE

In this chapter, we had a look at the following topics:

- iconic Japanese dishes and their significance
- recommended places to eat

As we wrap up this delicious journey through Japanese cuisine, let's not forget that the beauty of Japan lies not just in its popular destinations but also in its hidden gems. In the next chapter, we'll explore Japan's off-the-beaten-path treasures, where the heart and soul of the country truly reside. Join us in discovering the Japan that few get to experience.

7

EXPLORING JAPAN'S MUST-SEE ATTRACTIONS

Japan, a land of contrasts, offers a mesmerizing mix of modern cities and ancient traditions, bustling metropolises, and serene retreats. The country is made up of four primary islands: Hokkaido, Honshu, Shikoku, and Kyushu, along with numerous smaller islands.

Honshu is Japan's largest island, offering a popular travel route that unfolds from the eastern Kanto region, meanders through the central Chubu region, and culminates in the vibrant western Kansai region. Our journey will begin in Tokyo, the cornerstone of the Kanto region, continue through the historic core of Nagoya, a Chubu region highlight, and finally reach the bustling city of Osaka, the crowning jewel of Kansai. On this path, we'll explore one-of-a-kind attractions and cultural wonders in the neighboring areas.

KANTO REGION

Tokyo

Exploring Tokyo's Diversity in Harajuku and Shibuya

When exploring Tokyo, you simply can't miss the vibrant shopping districts of Harajuku and Shibuya. Spending a day immersing yourself in the vibrant atmospheres of these two areas is an absolute delight, and the best part is that they are conveniently just an eight-minute drive away. To commence your day, a visit to the Meiji Shrine, located near Harajuku Station, provides a serene and contemplative experience. This sacred site pays homage to Emperor Meiji and Empress Shoken and is situated in a vast 700,000 square meter forest with over 100,000 trees, providing a rejuvenating connection with nature.

Following your peaceful visit to the shrine, you can dive headfirst into the lively heart of Harajuku on Takeshita Street. Here, you'll encounter the latest fashion trends, unique treasures, and a vibrant blend of culture and cuisine embodying Tokyo's youthful spirit. As you explore this dynamic street, don't forget to savor local delights like cotton candy, cream puffs, and crepes.

Once you've thoroughly explored Takeshita Street, you can venture into Omotesando's upscale elegance and Cat Street's eclectic charm. Omotesando is home to luxury brands and iconic stores, while Cat Street offers a diverse range of well-known brands, contemporary labels, sportswear, and specialty shops. You might even stumble upon some charming hat boutiques. And, of course, no visit is complete without savoring the delicious pancakes at "bills."

As you wrap up your adventure in Harajuku, you can hop on the JR Yamanote Line to Shibuya. In addition to its fantastic shopping scene reminiscent of Harajuku's, Shibuya PARCO is a paradise for manga and anime enthusiasts. Here, you can immerse yourself in the captivating worlds of Pokémon Center Shibuya, Nintendo TOKYO, and the Jump Shop, all brimming with an enticing array of manga and anime collectibles.

When it's time for a well-deserved meal, you can head to Shibuya Nonbei Yokocho, a charming alley nestled beside the Shibuya train line. Here, you'll discover around 40 cozy izakayas (Japanese pubs), each with its unique atmosphere, offering an authentic dining experience.

To top off your day of exploration, make your way to Shibuya Sky and relish the mesmerizing Tokyo nightscape from its 360° open-air observation deck. The highlight of this experience is undoubtedly the exhilarating aerial escalator ride that provides breathtaking panoramic views of the city. It's a truly unforgettable way to conclude your memorable day in these vibrant Tokyo districts.

Appeasing Anime Enthusiasts in Akihabara and Ikebukuro

Tokyo is often considered an anime enthusiast's paradise, and two of its iconic hubs are Akihabara and Ikebukuro. Both locations are conveniently accessible via the JR Yamanote Line, making exploring them easy. In fact, given the plethora of anime-related offerings, dedicating a day to each place is an excellent idea for true enthusiasts.

Akihabara, affectionately known as "Akiba," is renowned for its overwhelming selection of anime merchandise. The area is a treasure trove of anime, gaming, and electronics shops. One standout destination is the Mandarake Complex, one of the largest anime shops globally, offering both modern and retro collectibles. If you're interested in electronics, Dospara Akihabara and Yodobashi Akihabara are worth a visit. Moreover, Akihabara is synonymous with cosplay culture, and you'll find many shops offering costumes, props, and materials. A must-visit spot is Akiba Zettai Ryōiki, a popular maid cafe where charming maids enhance your dining experience with their enchanting service, including drawing cute decorations on your meals.

Ikebukuro, not far from Akihabara, is another haven for anime aficionados. It boasts a multitude of shops catering to your every anime-related desire. The Animate flagship store is a significant attraction, offering a wide range of merchandise, from character goods to books, magazines, CDs, DVDs, games, and art supplies. You can also find one of the anime cafes mentioned in Chapter 6 within this flagship store but remember to make reservations in advance. Ikebukuro's unique feature is The Otome Road, or "The Maiden's Road," which is lined with shops primarily focusing on female-targeted anime and manga. Don't miss K-BOOKS, an expansive complex offering everything from anime and manga to character goods, doujinshi, and cosplay items.

For a distinctive experience, venture into the world of butler cafes in Ikebukuro. The Swallowtail Cafe, in particular, is highly recommended. Upon entering, you'll be greeted with a courteous "welcome home, princess" from well-trained butlers, enhancing your visit. Due to its popularity, it's advisable to make reservations at least ten days in advance, but you can also try your luck by visiting on the day itself.

Beyond the world of anime-related shops, Ikebukuro has an enchanting feature: the Toden Arakawa Line, also known as the "Tokyo Cherry Blossom Tram" for its scenic route along numerous cherry blossom viewing spots. It's Tokyo's only remaining public tram, spanning 30 stations between Minowabashi Station and Waseda Station, with Ikebukuro as the fifth stop from Waseda. The tram journey takes about 56 minutes and offers a glimpse of traditional Japanese culture and the charming "shitamachi" ambiance. After a day of anime exploration in

Ikebukuro, it's a peaceful way to unwind and soak in the serene surroundings.

Discovering Tokyo's Timeless Charm in Asakusa and Ueno

Have you ever been curious about the concept of Shitamachi? This term, translating to "lower town," encapsulates the traditional essence of Tokyo's neighborhoods. Its origins can be traced back to the geography of Edo, the city's ancient name. Notably, Asakusa and Ueno are two districts that vividly embody the shitamachi ambiance.

Exploring Asakusa starts just a stone's throw away from the train station, where the majestic Kaminarimon gate warmly welcomes visitors. This gate, dominated by a colossal red lantern adorned with the word "Kaminarimon," serves as a symbol of protection, guarded by the God of Thunder on the left and the God of Wind on the right. These deities are revered for safeguarding the Asakusa Temple from calamities, embodying benevolence.

On the other side of the Kaminarimon gate is the Nakamise shopping street, embellished with 89 diverse shops. While the term "Nakamise" is commonly associated with shopping streets located within temple or shrine compounds, this particular alley stands out as one of the oldest ones in Japan. It offers an array of souvenirs and a taste of Tokyo's classic street food. The path eventually guides you to one of Tokyo's oldest temples, the illustrious Sensoji Temple. With a rich history spanning 1,400 years, it's a place of reverence for Kannon, the Buddhist goddess of mercy. This temple attracts millions of pilgrims and tourists each year.

For a more immersive experience of Shitamachi's charm, a five-minute journey on the Tokyo Metro Ginza Line will transport you to Ueno. Here, you'll encounter the bustling Ameya-Yokocho market, stretching approximately 437 yards and offering various goods, from affordable delicacies and stylish bags to clothing and cosmetics. The energetic vendors enthusiastically promoting their affordable prices truly immerse you in the authentic Shitamachi atmosphere.

After your exploration of Ameya-Yokocho, a short train ride or 40-minute walk will introduce you to Yanaka Ginza, a boulevard that resonates with the spirit of the Edo era. Originating during the Showa era with the intention of supporting the local community, this area has naturally evolved into a bustling commercial hub, now housing over 60 stores. Interestingly, Yanaka Ginza is also known as "Cat Street." As you stroll along its charming streets, you'll likely encounter cats leisurely lounging and playfully wandering about, adding to the relaxed and nostalgic Shitamachi atmosphere.

Immersing Yourself in Tokyo's Many Museums

Tokyo offers an array of museums and art galleries, making it a prime destination for people of all interests. Within this realm of diverse options, I'd like to spotlight two exceptional venues: Miraikan and the Ghibli Museum.

Miraikan, officially known as "The National Museum of Emerging Science and Innovation," stands as a beacon of technological progress in Odaiba. This museum focuses on space exploration, robotics, and cutting-edge technologies, earning it the moniker "the museum of the future." Its dynamic nature is reflected in the ever-changing special exhibitions it hosts. In the past, these have included captivating showcases inspired by popular series like the "Pokémon Research Institute" and "Detective Conan." To explore this extraordinary museum, you can conveniently purchase tickets on-site. However, keep in mind that Miraikan is closed on Tuesdays, so plan your visit accordingly.

On the other hand, for ardent fans of Studio Ghibli, the Ghibli Museum is definitely worth a visit! Conceived and designed by the legendary Hayao Miyazaki, this enchanting museum opened its doors to the public in 2001. Miyazaki's vision transcends mere fandom, as he aims to ignite a profound passion and appreciation for the art of animation in every visitor. To experience it yourself, be sure to book your tickets in advance. These can be secured through the official museum website or via the JTB Group Overseas. Due to its immense popularity, tickets tend to sell out incredibly quickly once they're available online. However, there's a silver lining for fans—the new Ghibli Park, which opened its doors in 2022, provides an additional opportunity to immerse yourself in all things Ghibli. We'll delve deeper into this enchanting park in our upcoming Nagoya section.

CHŪBU REGION

After indulging in the marvels of Tokyo, it's time to journey westward. The Tokaido Shinkansen provides a seamless link, connecting the Kanto region's Tokyo to Kansai's Osaka. But before we dive into the enchantments of Kansai, let's take a moment to immerse ourselves fully in the heart of Honshu. Nagoya, proudly positioned as the core of this region, stands as one of Japan's three mega-cities, forming a formidable trio alongside Tokyo and Osaka.

Nagoya

Nagoya unveils a rich historical heritage, having played a prominent role in the narratives of numerous legendary figures in Japanese history. Among these figures, the renowned "Three Heroes of the Warring States"—Oda Nobunaga, Toyotomi Hideyoshi, and Tokugawa Ieyasu—have left an indelible mark on this city, bestowing upon it a treasury of historical landmarks and attractions.

The most illustrious gem among these attractions is the Nagoya Castle. This grand citadel, commissioned by the unifying shogun, Tokugawa Ieyasu, in 1615, stands as a testament to architectural brilliance. Crowned with resplendent golden shachihoko—the iconic tiger-fish roof ornaments—the castle boasts a sprawling interior within its tower keep, accompanied by the magnificent Hommaru Palace. Beyond its architectural splendor, this fortress once served as a pivotal military stronghold. Despite the scars of wartime air raids that marred its magnificence, the profound historical significance of Nagoya Castle has earned it the prestigious designation as a National Historic Site.

Venturing into the lively shopping boulevards surrounding the Osukannon and Banshoji temples, visitors can revel in an enchanting blend of old-world charm and modern vitality. Echoing the vibrancy of the Edo era, the Osu Shopping District beckons with open arms, especially after you've explored the Osukannon Temple. Stretching over 1859 yards, this covered shopping arcade hosts a treasure trove of over 1,200 shops offering a diverse array of products. Notably, it has emerged as a hub for otaku culture and holds the distinction of being the birthplace of cosplay, serving as the stage for the annual World Cosplay Summit.

For those enchanted by the magic of Studio Ghibli, the newly inaugurated Ghibli Park in 2022 is an absolute must-visit. A mere 40-minute Meitetsu shuttle bus journey from Nagoya Station to Ai-Chikyuhaku Kinen Koen will transport you to this whimsical world. By 2023, this fantastical space had flourished into five distinct realms, each telling a unique Ghibli tale. However, it's worth noting that, akin to the Ghibli Museum, spontaneity won't suffice when securing tickets; advanced online reservations are a must.

Takayama

Takayama, also known formally as Hida-Takayama, is a hidden gem located in the heart of central Honshu, inviting exploration. The journey to Takayama from Nagoya via the JR Hida Limited Express is a journey in itself, taking approximately two and a half hours. This train route is renowned for its breathtaking scenic beauty. It has earned the nickname "Wide View Hida" due to its expansive windows offering panoramic views of the captivating countryside and well-preserved historic landmarks.

The soul of Takayama lies in its rich historical heritage. The town is compact and walkable, making it almost impossible to lose your way. A mere 15-minute walk from the JR station leads you to Sanmachi-dori, an ancient quarter that transports you back to the Edo period. While you meander through its charming streets, admiring the historic architecture, you'll also encounter a plethora of restaurants and cafes showcasing local cuisine and products. For aficionados of beef, sampling the local specialty, Hida beef, is a must, and Hida beef sushi stands out as a delightful dish worth trying.

Taking a little further journey, you'll reach the Hida Folk Village. Located about 15 minutes away from Takayama station by bus, this open-air museum boasts a collection of over 30 traditional houses dating back to the Edo Period. Among these preserved structures, you'll find storage buildings, logging cabins, and the residence of the former village head. The architecture of these buildings has earned them the name "Gassho village," owing to their steep thatched roofs that resemble hands joined in prayer ("gassho").

Should you decide to spend the night in Takayama, make sure to visit Miyagawa Morning Market, situated alongside the Miyagawa River in the old town. While wandering through this lively market, you'll be enticed by fresh produce, handmade crafts, pickles, miso, and various other local Hida specialties. Beyond its role as a shopping haven, it provides a unique opportunity to connect with the locals, with the stall owners' warmth and hospitality offering a glimpse into the local culture.

KANSAI REGION

After exploring the central region, we'll journey west from Nagoya station aboard the Tokaido Shinkansen. However, a truly enchanting destination awaits us before we reach Osaka: Kyoto. This city, once the heartbeat of Japan, boasts a history that stretches back over a thousand years, making it a guardian of Japan's timeless and cherished traditional culture.

Kyoto

Kyoto boasts a staggering array of over 1,600 temples, underlining its spiritual significance. If you're eager to explore these temples but uncertain about where to begin, let me point you in the direction of three exceptional ones.

Kiyomizudera stands as one of Kyoto's most ancient and awe-inspiring temples. This sacred site, dedicated to the deity thousand-armed Kannon, sits atop a small hill to the east of Kyoto. Its remarkable wooden stage, elevated 43 feet above the hillside, sets it apart and offers breathtaking views of the cherry and maple trees that envelop it. This view is especially captivating during the vibrant spring cherry blossoms and the rich autumn foliage. What's more, during the spring, summer, and autumn seasons, the temple opens its doors for evening visits when it's softly illuminated, revealing a different kind of beauty under the night sky. As you explore, you'll also find stone-paved pathways that harken back to ancient Kyoto, leading you to charming stalls offering unique souvenirs and local snacks.

A 20-minute walk from these pathways, particularly from Sannen-zaka, nenenomichi, ichinen-zaka, and ninen-zaka, will lead you to Yasaka Shrine, affectionately known as Gion-san by the locals. It's one of Kyoto's most visited shrines, dedicated to Susano-o, a heroic deity renowned for saving a maiden from the clutches of an eight-headed serpent and later marrying her. This shrine is especially famous for hosting the Gion Matsuri festival every summer in July. Historically, Yasaka Shrine bore the name Gion Shrine, which lent its name to the iconic historical district of Kyoto, Gion. Once a shrine town during the Edo era, Gion has gradually evolved into an area of entertainment and cultural significance. Today, Gion extends beyond a single street, encompassing shopping lanes, upscale restaurants, residential areas, and the world-famous geisha district. It's particularly celebrated for its captivating Kabuki performances and the enigmatic world of geishas.

Before losing yourself in Gion's enchanting depths, stroll along Shijo-dori. This lively shopping street is brimming with a variety of Kyoto's culinary delights and souvenirs. Afterward, don't forget to visit Hanami-koji, Gion's most renowned street. Here, stone-paved pathways wind their way through Edo-period buildings and quaint teahouses reminiscent of ancient Kyoto. If you're lucky, you might catch a glimpse of a geisha on her way to an engagement. These "women of the arts" undergo rigorous training in music, dance, and art. Please note that photographing a geisha without her consent is prohibited.

Finally, Fushimi Inari Taisha is an essential destination to visit. This shrine is famed for its thousands of striking vermilion torii gates that line the pathways leading through the shrine. These paths eventually lead you into the serene forests of Mount Inari, a sacred peak within the shrine's sprawling grounds. Fushimi Inari Taisha is the chief among many shrines dedicated to Inari, the Shinto deity associated with rice. Throughout the shrine, you'll encounter numerous fox statues, regarded as divine messengers of Inari.

Aside from its revered temples and shrines, Kyoto is a city of historical splendor. Nijo Castle, for instance, stands as a splendid example. This magnificent castle was commissioned by Tokugawa Ieyasu, the same visionary behind Nagoya Castle, who played a pivotal role in unifying Japan, ending the turbulent Warring States period, and ushering in the prosperous Edo era. Spanning 275,000 square meters, Nijo Castle, fortified by dual moats surrounding its central structures, is a testament to architectural grandeur. It offers visitors a captivating journey through history and the opportunity to explore its exquisite gardens.

Beyond its historical landmarks, Kyoto is renowned for its natural beauty, with the famous towering bamboo groves nestled in the enchanting Sagano Bamboo Forest in Arashiyama. While there are numerous routes to reach Arashiyama, I highly recommend the Sagano Scenic Railway, which treats you to captivating views of the riverside and rolling hills.

Nara

On your way to Osaka, I recommend taking a detour to Nara, an ancient capital located just south of Kyoto. Here, you'll be greeted by the iconic deer that has become a symbol of Japan. These friendly creatures are renowned for their charming bows to passersby.

Nara hosts an array of ancient Buddhist temples reminiscent of Kyoto's grandeur. Many travelers intentionally make a stop here to witness Nara's renowned Great Buddha and the lovable deer that call this place home. One of the most distinguished temples in Nara is Todai-ji, situated right next to Nara Park. The 50-foot-tall Buddha enshrined within Todai-ji, along with the temple itself, holds the esteemed status of a national treasure in Japan. Moreover, Todai-ji boasts the remarkable distinction of being the world's largest wooden building.

After you've marveled at the wonders of Todai-ji, interact with the deer that reside in Nara Park by feeding them "shika senbei" (deer crackers). Around 1,000 deer roam freely in this area, deeply ingrained in the culture and history of the region. Nara Park is quite extensive, and besides Todai-ji, you can conveniently reach another prominent attraction, Kasuga Taisha Shrine, with just a short stroll. If you require a little rest, you'll find numerous restaurants near Nara Park that offer a chance to savor local cuisine.

It's also worth noting that if you find yourself with some spare time in Nara, you might consider a half-day excursion to Uji, which is easily accessible via the JR Nara Line, as mentioned in Chapter 6. The journey to Uji takes approximately 50 minutes from Nara JR Station, and it's a great way to explore even more of the beautiful Kansai region.

Osaka

Now, let's hop back on the Tokaido Shinkansen and continue our journey from Kyoto to Osaka. With a quick 30-minute ride, you'll find yourself at Shin-Osaka Station, marking your entry into vibrant Osaka.

If you're eager to explore the shopping scene and dive into the local culture of Osaka, make your way to Namba. It's a mere 20-minute ride from Shin-Osaka station. Once you arrive at Namba Station, a two-minute walk will take you to the EbisuBashi Shopping Street. From there, you can wander all the way to Dotonbori and Shinsaibashi Shopping Street. Along this route, you'll encounter a wealth of shops offering a wide range of goods and a diverse array of authentic local cuisine. If you happen to be a fan of crab, make sure not to miss the Kani Doraku Dotonbori Main Branch in Dotonbori, easily recognizable by its giant king crab sign. This restaurant specializes in crab dishes, offering an extensive selection of crab-focused sets, from crab tempura to grilled dishes, sashimi, hotpot, and more.

For a change of pace from the bustling city center, I recommend a visit to Hozenji Yokocho, a tranquil alley just a three-minute walk from the Dotonbori district. This roughly 80-meter-long stone-paved alleyway is adorned with old-style Japanese open-air shops, traditional cafes, restaurants, and izakayas. As the night falls, lanterns illuminate the area, creating a magical ambiance that transports you to a different world and era.

In addition to your shopping and culinary delights, Osaka is home to one of Japan's three historically significant castles, Osaka Castle. Located in the heart of the city, the castle serves as a symbol of Osaka. Its construction began in 1583 under the leadership of Toyotomi Hideyoshi. Over time, the castle has witnessed numerous conflicts, undergoing destruction and reconstruction multiple times. The present-day Osaka Castle, reconstructed in 1931, now stands as a museum with a five-story facade and eight interior floors. It is surrounded by the vast Osaka Castle Park, a renowned cherry blossom viewing spot in spring. Beyond the park lies a wide outer moat, offering travelers scenic boat tours that provide an alternative perspective of the castle's grandeur.

For breathtaking views of Osaka, be sure not to miss the Abeno Harukas 300 Observatory. Soaring 984 feet above the ground, Abeno Harukas proudly holds the title of

Japan's tallest building, with the Abeno Harukas Observatory perched at its zenith. From this vantage point, you can relish panoramic vistas of bustling Osaka, catching glimpses of Kyoto, the Rokko Mountain Range in Kobe, and other areas in the Kansai region.

Lastly, I'd like to recommend Universal Studios Japan (USJ). Much like Tokyo's Disneyland, Osaka boasts Universal Studios, each with its unique charm. In particular, "The Wizarding World of Harry Potter" and "Super Nintendo World" are immensely popular attractions. USJ frequently collaborates with beloved manga and anime franchises. For instance, it hosted the "One Piece Premier Summer 2023" event, featuring One Piece musical performances and Sanji's Pirates Restaurant. These collaborations with beloved manga works are a distinctive highlight of USJ. While it's not mandatory, I highly recommend purchasing your USJ tickets online to bypass long lines at the park entrance.

TO SUMMARIZE

In this chapter, we explored a few highly recommended attractions in the following regions:

- Kanto
- Chūbu
- Kansai

As you immerse yourself in everything these regions have to offer, always keep in mind that unforeseen surprises can disrupt even the most meticulously crafted plans. Adaptability and resourcefulness are your best allies, whether it's an unexpected rainstorm, a misplaced wallet, or a missed train.

Join us in the upcoming section, where we'll delve into common travel challenges and provide you with practical solutions for addressing them. Get ready to explore the tools and insights that will keep you well-prepared and enable you to seize the opportunities presented by every situation during your Japanese adventure.

8

EMBRACING THE UNPLANNED–GUIDE TO UNEXPECTED ADVENTURES IN JAPAN

Even meticulously planned journeys can encounter unexpected setbacks. For example, you may find yourself on a stroll through the streets of Kyoto, savoring the sight of beautiful cherry blossoms, when, out of the blue, a heavy downpour unleashes its fury. The downpour catches you off guard, and you realize you're a considerable distance from your hotel, plus you didn't have the foresight to bring an umbrella. What will you do? Such unforeseen situations and how to deal with them are exactly what we'll cover in this chapter. So, let's dive in!

INTRODUCING COMMON TRAVEL CHALLENGES

Communication Hurdles With Local Residents

One of the most prominent hurdles travelers face in Japan is the language barrier. While major cities and tourist destinations often have some English signage and people who speak English, you'll frequently encounter people who are more comfortable conversing in Japanese. Carrying a translation app or learning some basic Japanese phrases can go a long way in bridging this gap and making your journey smoother.

Shortage of Multilingual Maps, Signs, and Tourism Materials

One notable challenge that foreign travelers often encounter in Japan is the scarcity of multilingual maps, signs, and tourism materials. This gap in multilingual support can lead to difficulties in comprehending essential information such as directions, landmarks, and local customs, which can leave you feeling disoriented. Luckily, Japanese train stations and tourist hubs have volunteer guides who speak multiple languages, helping navigate Japan's less English-friendly areas.

Exits are Difficult to Find

Navigating through Japan's extensive train stations and complex shopping malls, you might find that exits are not always as straightforward as you'd expect. Multiple entrances, numerous floors, and a lack of clear signage can make finding your way out a bit challenging. Consider using smartphone apps, station maps, or asking station staff or fellow travelers for assistance to ease the process. Staying patient and allowing extra time to locate your exit will help prevent unnecessary stress during your travels.

It's Easy to Get Lost

Japan's intricate urban landscapes and winding rural streets can sometimes make it easy to get lost, even with the best navigation tools. Therefore, try to familiarize yourself with nearby landmarks, railway stations, or street signs to maintain your sense of direction, and always carry a mobile device with GPS to ensure you can find your way back to your destination.

Inconspicuous/Scarcity of Smoking Zones in Japan

In Japan, travelers and residents alike often encounter a notable challenge in the form of inconspicuous and scarce smoking zones. Stringent smoking regulations have led to a scarcity of designated smoking areas, especially in urban and public spaces. While designated zones exist, they can be challenging to find, and they may be relatively small. Smokers are encouraged to be mindful of local regulations and inquire about the nearest smoking areas to ensure a smooth and respectful experience while navigating this challenge in Japan.

Rain is Inevitable

Travelers exploring Japan should be prepared for unexpected rain during their journey. Rainfall is a common occurrence in Japan, and the weather can change rapidly, especially during the rainy season or in coastal regions. If you find yourself caught in an unexpected rain shower, it's a good idea to take refuge in a nearby store or cafe. Numerous convenience stores in Japan offer affordable umbrellas for sale, making it easy to acquire one if you need to venture out in wet weather. Alternatively, you can opt for a cozy break in a local café while waiting for the rain to subside.

EXTRA PRECAUTIONS TO TAKE

Be Aware of the Weather

When it comes to packing for your trip, it's essential to stay informed about the weather conditions in the specific regions of Japan you plan to explore. Japan's climate varies significantly from one area to another, and failing to do a bit of research can lead to unexpected weather-related surprises. For instance, winters in Hokkaido can be exceedingly frigid, while summers in Japan, particularly in cities like Tokyo, can be oppressively hot and humid. It's also crucial to determine whether your visit coincides with Japan's rainy season or if you might encounter the occasional typhoon. Being aware of these weather patterns is invaluable when it comes to deciding what to pack. Depending on your home country, you might find the Japanese climate markedly different from what you initially anticipated!

Don't Overbook Your Itinerary

While it's undeniable that Japan boasts a multitude of captivating cities worth exploring, it's essential to consider how much of any city you can truly experience in just one or two days, factoring in travel time. Undoubtedly, you'll need to make some tough choices and exclude some fantastic options, but in doing so, you'll find that your journey becomes more fulfilling.

Especially if you relish connecting with the locals and aspire to explore those hidden gems that many tourists never have the chance to see, shift your focus from tallying up cities visited to the depth of your understanding of each place you've ventured into. Most travelers prefer to explore two or three cities, especially on their first trip. Some even go as far as dedicating their entire vacation to a single town. Ultimately, the choice is yours, but if feasible, aim to extend your stay in Japan for as long as your schedule allows. The longer you stay, the more profound and enriching your experience will become.

Avoid Overpacking

When it comes to packing for your trip, try not to load up on too many clothing items, even if your visit extends over a longer period. No matter your interests, whether it's anime, quirky gadgets, unique snacks, fashion, traditional crafts, or ornamental pieces, Japan boasts its unique rendition of them all, and you'll need the extra space to bring back all the goods you bought during your travels. Additionally, most accommodations in Japan offer laundry facilities, and you'll often come across coin-operated self-service laundromats so you can keep recycling the clothes you brought. It's also worth noting that certain train stations may lack escalators or elevators. This makes lugging around bulky suitcases, or multiple ones, a less-than-ideal choice.

Bring Comfortable Shoes

Exploring new cities often requires a fair amount of walking and, in many cases, more than we're used to. Yet, certain days in Japan can put even seasoned travelers to the test when it comes to getting around on foot. With so much to see and so little time, Japan's transportation system is excellent, but sometimes it's more efficient to walk from one place to another, and it can even save you money if you're traveling on a budget.

While a 20-minute or half-hour walk to your next destination may not seem like much, when you do this several times a day, those minutes and miles quickly add up. Those of us mindful of staying active might even find ourselves averaging around 10,000 to 15,000 steps per day. Your choice of comfortable footwear will ultimately determine whether you end up confined to your hotel bed the next day or ready for another round of exploration in the morning.

Plan for Hypotheticals

One aspect that travelers often tend to overlook, and something they might later regret not considering, is the necessity of medical or travel insurance. Depending on your country of origin, you'll likely find numerous companies offering such services. With a bit of research, you'll be able to find a few affordable options that can ultimately prove to be a genuine money-saver, not to mention a source of peace of mind. Regardless of your travel destination around the world, being prepared is always a wise choice.

In the case of Japan, for instance, the cost of a doctor's visit or, in more severe situations, hospitalization can amount to a significant expense. Prolonged hospital stays can quickly accumulate substantial costs. Hopefully, you won't find yourself needing to use your insurance. However, especially if you're traveling with children, it's highly advisable to prioritize this insurance as a vital component of your pre-trip preparations.

Book in Advance

You'd be surprised how often it's necessary to book in advance during your trip to Japan. Booking popular restaurants, for example, can be quite a task, as you may have to do so several weeks in advance to secure a table. Of course, this doesn't mean you have to book a table for every restaurant you want to dine at. Most places are perfectly fine for walk-ins. However, if you're planning to visit a restaurant with a Michelin star or one that's highly acclaimed, it's a good idea to avoid long waiting times by reserving in advance. In Japan, when something is popular it can get crowded very quickly. Considering that planning well ahead is a common practice among Japanese locals, it can be a bit challenging for those of us who prefer spontaneous plans.

Pack Small Gifts for Others

This might seem a bit unconventional. When traveling abroad, the focus is often on purchasing souvenirs for friends and family back home, and we rarely think about small gifts for people we might encounter during our journey. However, this tip comes in handy when you're exploring Japan. You might already know some locals, or you could strike up new friendships along the way. It's not uncommon to form connections with people you meet at a bar, restaurant, or while wandering the streets.

Frequently, your Japanese friends might traditionally present you with a small keepsake to remember them and your time in the country before you depart. If you're staying at a bed and breakfast with a local family or at a guest house with fellow travelers, receiving some tokens of appreciation is almost expected. So, why not reciprocate the kindness by giving them a gift from your own country? No one will anticipate a gift from you, and no one would think any less of you if you haven't thought of it, but if you do, it will undoubtedly create an even more heartwarming memory of you for the people you've met.

ESSENTIAL CONTACTS AND RESOURCES

Police: 110

If you're the victim of a crime or need to report one, it's essential to contact the police to document the incident for both legal and insurance reasons. Similarly, in the case of a minor traffic accident, dialing 110 is the appropriate course of action.

Ambulance or Fire Department: 119

If you encounter a fire or require immediate medical assistance, call 119. While some support for English and a few other foreign languages is available (connecting you to a third-party interpreter), it may introduce delays. Therefore, it's advisable to learn some essential Japanese phrases, such as "kyuukyuu desu" which means "It's a medical emergency" when you need an ambulance, and "kaji desu" for fire.

Non-Urgent Medical: #7119

If you or someone is unwell or injured, and you're uncertain whether an ambulance is necessary, you can dial #7119 for assistance. This helpline can provide guidance and advice on the best course of action.

Coast Guard: 118

If you encounter a maritime emergency within Japanese waters, you can reach out to the Japanese Coast Guard by dialing 118. They are equipped to provide swift assistance and support in such situations.

Disaster Line: 171

In the event of a disaster like an earthquake, you have the option to use NTT's Web 171 service to inform your loved ones back home of your well-being. However, if you have internet access, it's often more convenient to send an email or post a quick message on social media that you're safe.

If you made any new friends or have family in Japan, you can use the 171 Disaster Line, which is accessible only to domestic (Japanese) telephone numbers. The line functions as a message board for recording voice messages that automatically notify them. To record a voice message, follow these steps:

1. Dial 171.
2. Press 1, followed by the phone number of your family member.

To listen to your message, the recipient needs to:

1. Dial 171.
2. Press 2, followed by their phone number.

Support in English

When reaching out to emergency services for the police, ambulance, or fire department, expect the initial response to be in Japanese, with a possibility that the operator might only comprehend Japanese. Nevertheless, assistance in various languages is available through third-party interpreters who can be connected. The specific languages supported may vary by municipality, but English is commonly among the supported languages, providing reassurance for English-speaking travelers.

JAPAN'S SAFETY AND SECURITY

Japan is frequently hailed as one of the safest countries globally, and it's a place where people often feel comfortable enough to doze off on trains or at stations. It's not uncommon to see passengers leaving their bags ajar or their phones resting on their laps, and remarkably, incidents of theft are exceedingly rare. To illustrate Japan's safety, a popular example often used is that if you lose your wallet in Japan, it will be returned to you. Surprisingly, this statement is not a myth.

A report from the Tokyo Metropolitan Police Department revealed that in 2017, the police received almost 4 million reports of found items, while only around a million reports were filed for lost items (*Live Japan,* 2019c). That makes the number of found items turned over to the police approximately four times greater than the number of reports for lost items. This suggests that a considerable number of people not only report found items to the police but also hand in items that owners may have abandoned their search for.

Additionally, Japan's Lost Goods Law legally mandates individuals who discover lost items to promptly submit it to the police or return the lost item to its owner. After the owner has reclaimed the item, they are obliged to reward the finder, offering no less than five percent and no more than 20% of the item's estimated value. However, many Japanese citizens may not be aware of the specifics regarding these reward rules, and in most instances, they won't request rewards since their actions are motivated by goodwill.

TO SUMMARIZE

In this chapter, we explored the following:

- common travel challenges
- extra precautions to take to ensure a smooth travel experience

- essential contacts and resources in case of emergencies
- Japan's superior safety and security

As you explore the wonders of Japan, being prepared for the unexpected can help you navigate any challenges that come your way. You've now learned practical strategies for handling common travel issues and how to be resourceful in unforeseen circumstances. In the next chapter, we'll explore a few essential phrases that will certainly come in handy as you journey through Japan.

BONUS CHAPTER: LOST IN TRANSLATION? JAPANESE PHRASES TO THE RESCUE!

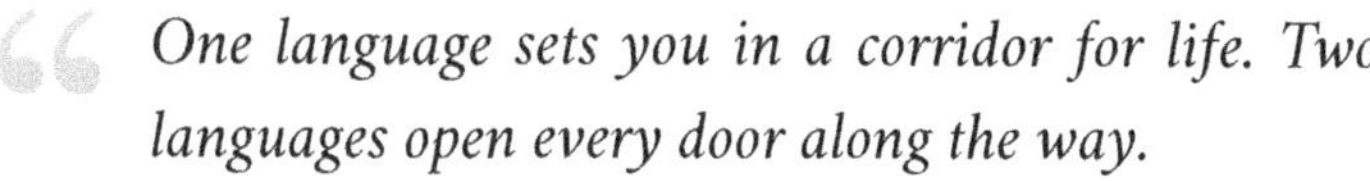

> *One language sets you in a corridor for life. Two languages open every door along the way.*
>
> — FRANK SMITH

BASIC JAPANESE PHRASES AND THEIR PRONUNCIATION

The prospect of talking to a native Japanese speaker can feel quite intimidating. I've certainly experienced that feeling myself, and I'm sure you might worry that they won't understand you or that you'll lack the vocabulary to express your thoughts. The good news is that I've compiled a comprehensive list of useful Japanese phrases so you can confidently enter your first conversation.

Essential Words and Phrases

- **yes:** *hai* (はい。)
- **no:** *Iie* (いいえ。)
- **please:** *onegai shimasu* (おねがいします。)
- **thank you:** *arigatō* (ありがとう。)
- **you're welcome:** *doitashimashite* (どういたしまして。)
- **I'm sorry:** *gomennasai* (ごめんなさい。)
- **excuse me:** *sumimasen* (すみません。)

Greetings

- **hello:** *konnichiwa* (こんにちは)
- **goodbye:** *ja ne* (じゃね)
- **good morning:** *ohayou gozaimasu* (おはようございます)
- **good evening:** *konbanwa* (こんばんは)
- **good night:** *oyasumi nasai* (おやすみなさい。)
- **how are you:** *ogenki desu ka?* (お元気ですか)
- **I'm well:** *genki desu* (元気です)
- **long time no see:** *ohisashiburi desu* (お久しぶりです)

Crucial Questions

- **why:** *doushite?* (どうして)
- **when is it:** *itsu desu ka?* (いつですか)
- **where is it:** *doko desu ka?* (どこですか)

- **who is it:** *dare desu ka?* (だれですか)
- **what is it:** *nan desu ka?* (何ですか)
- **what is that:** *sore wa nan desu ka?* (それはなんですか)
- **what is this:** *kore wa nan desu ka?* (これはなんですか)
- **which one is it:** *dochira desu ka?* (どちらですか)
- **how much does that cost:** *Ikura desu ka?* (いくらですか)

Asking for Clarification

- **can you help me:** *tetsudatte kuremasen ka?* (手伝ってくれませんか)
- **I don't understand:** *wakarimasen* (わかりません)
- **could you say that again:** *mou ichido itte kudasai* (もう一度言ってください)
- **please go a little slower:** *motto yukkuri kudasai* (もっとゆっくり下さい)
- **what does ___ mean:** ___ *tte dou iu imi desuka* (__ってどういう意味ですか)
- **and in English, that's...:** *eigo te iu no wa...* (英語ていうのは)
- **I'm not very fluent in Japanese:** *watashi wa nihongo ga amari umaku naidesu* (私は日本語があまり上手ないです)
- **I don't know:** *shirimasen* (知りません)
- **I forgot:** *wasuremashita* (忘れました)

Conversational Phrases

- **my name is ___:** *watashi no namae wa ___ desu* (私の名前は___です)
- **what's your name:** *namae wa nan desu ka?* (名前は何ですか)
- **I'm from ___:** *watashi wa ___ kara kimashita* (私は___から来ました)
- **where are you from:** *doko kara kimashita ka?* (どこから来ましたか)
- **really?/Is that so?/I see:** *sou desu ka?* (そうですか)

When Dining

- **I humbly receive:** *itadakimasu* (いただきます)
- **bon appetit:** *meshiagare* (召し上がれ)
- **it was a feast:** *gochisousama deshita* （ごちそうさまでした)
- **cheers:** *kanpai* (カンパイ)
- **this is delicious:** *oishii* (美味しい)
- **do you have an English menu:** *eigo no menyū wa arimasu ka?* (英語のメニューはありますか。)
- **what is today's special:** *kyō no osusume wa nan desu ka?* (今日のおすすめは何ですか。)

In Case of an Emergency

- **help me:** *tasukete* (助けて)
- **please call an ambulance:** *kyuu kyuusha o yonde kudasai* (救急車を呼んで下さい)
- **please call the police:** *keisatsu o yonde kudasai* (警察を呼んで下さい)

POLITENESS AND FORMALITY IN SPEECH

In Japanese, there are distinct language styles for every social situation, incorporating various levels of formality directly into their grammar. Depending on their relationship with the person they're communicating with, Japanese speakers adjust their language to demonstrate the appropriate level of respect.

Similar to English speakers, they select specific words and structure their sentences differently. Still, unlike languages lacking distinct formal registers, they even alter verb forms based on the required politeness level. During a first introduction, using the right level of formality can convey a lot about yourself and leave either a positive impression or an unfortunate blunder.

Honorifics

The first technique to infuse your speech with politeness is honorifics. The honorific prefix "お" (pronounced as "o") is employed to express respect or politeness, particularly when referring to items associated with the listener. For instance, when referring to something of cultural significance like a temple or sake, you'll say "o-tera" or "o-sake." Similarly, when asking for someone's name, you'll say "o-namae". In some instances, this prefix essentially becomes an integral part of the word, as seen in "ocha" (tea).

A counterpart to "o" is the prefix "ご" (pronounced "go"), found in words like "gohan" (cooked rice), where the honorific is essentially inseparable from the root word. So, what distinguishes the two? Primarily, "o" is typically used for words of Japanese origin, while "go" is favored for words of Chinese origin.

Mastering the use of "o" and "go" may seem intricate. When dealing with words that invariably incorporate these prefixes, we treat them as an inherent part of the word. You'll develop an instinct for when to apply them to words that occasionally feature the prefix.

Formality Levels

In Japanese, there are four fundamental categories: casual, "teineigo," "sonkeigo," and "kenjougo." Navigating these categories is crucial, as choosing the right one depends on your familiarity with the person you're addressing and the nature of your relationship. Even when expressing gratitude with a simple "thank you," it's essential to use the appropriate level. To avoid any potential awkwardness in conversations, let's explore the rules for each tier of honorific Japanese and when to use which.

Casual Japanese

The guidelines for honorific Japanese revolve around two key factors: seniority or experience and the concept of 内外 (うちそと, uchi soto), which translates to "inside" and "outside." Typically, if someone is your age or younger or belongs to your personal social circle (uchi), you can comfortably engage in casual Japanese conversation. In casual Japanese, slang words are fair game; you may replace -です (-desu) with -だ (-da), and if you're a male speaker, you can use 俺 (おれ, ore) to refer to yourself. However, it's best to avoid using casual Japanese with noticeably older or more experienced individuals, especially when you've just met them.

Teineigo (Polite Form)

Teineigo represents the fundamental polite form of Japanese, often found in textbooks, and a safe choice when you're unsure about the appropriate level of politeness to use. Teineigo can be applied in workplace settings, when addressing strangers or new acquaintances of any age, and even within your immediate social circle.

In its basic form, teineigo entails adding the suffixes -です/-ます (-desu/-masu) to the ends of sentences or verbs, and using 私 (わたし、watashi) to refer to oneself. The only scenario in which teineigo might not be the best choice is when you're conversing with someone who shares a close relationship with you. In such cases, it could come across as overly formal, stiff, or unfriendly.

Sonkeigo (Honorific Form)

Sonkeigo is a form of language that shows great respect to the person you are addressing. This particular level of politeness is commonly employed in formal or business contexts, especially when conversing with individuals of higher rank or social status. For instance, when communicating with your company president or superiors, you would typically employ sonkeigo.

Unlike teineigo, sonkeigo doesn't follow a strict grammatical rule or formula. Instead, it introduces polite variations of casual or teineigo Japanese words. A basic example of this transition involves the teineigo form 食べます (たべます、tabemasu), meaning "to eat," which transforms into its sonkeigo counterpart 召し上がる (めしあがる、meshi agaru).

Kenjougo (Humble Form)

The humble form, kenjougo doesn't necessarily signify greater politeness compared to sonkeigo; rather, it serves a distinct purpose. While sonkeigo is employed to show respect to the person you are addressing, kenjougo is used to humble oneself as the speaker. It is designed to convey humility; consequently, kenjougo is unsuitable for use when referring to others as the subject of the sentence.

Similar to sonkeigo, the Japanese humble form involves its own set of polite language. It is frequently used in the customer service industry, where staff or servers adopt a humble approach when conversing with guests.

TO SUMMARIZE

In this chapter, we had a look at:

- basic Japanese phrases and their pronunciation
- politeness and formality in speech

Having some Japanese language essentials under your belt will come in handy as you travel through Japan. At the conclusion of this guide, we'll wrap up all the topics discussed and offer some final thoughts on how to make the most of your unforgettable journey through Japan.

Make It Easy for a Fellow Traveler!

You're ready to embark on the adventure of a lifetime. Take a moment to share the joy with a fellow traveler!

Simply by sharing your honest opinion of this book and a little about your own experience, you'll show new readers exactly where to find the guidebook they're looking for.

LEAVE A REVIEW!

Thank you so much for your support – and have an amazing trip!

Scan the QR code below to leave your review!

CONCLUSION

As we reach this book's final pages, you're now equipped with the keys to unlock an incredible traveling experience in Japan. Your journey is about to become an immersive experience where you'll not only see Japan but truly feel and understand it. Soon, you'll find yourself easily navigating this amazing country's intricacies with ease.

Let's take a moment to reflect on the challenges you might have faced before picking up this book. It's important to recognize how far you've come since then, armed with valuable knowledge and insights, to conquer these common pain points.

Remember when Japan's language barrier felt like a daunting obstacle? You might have worried about communicating with locals, understanding signs, or deciphering menus. But now, you've unlocked strategies to navigate this linguistic challenge. You're equipped with essential Japanese phrases and the confidence to venture beyond the English-speaking enclaves.

Then there's Japan's rich culture that comes with intricate social norms and etiquette. It might have seemed like a cultural minefield where unintentional missteps could lead to awkward situations and misunderstandings. But worry not; you've immersed yourself in the cultural nuances of Japan. You're well-prepared to respect local customs and interact with authenticity.

Additionally, the notion of Japan's high cost of living may have once sent budgeting jitters down your spine. You might have feared that unexpected expenses could jeopardize your travel experiences. However, you've now mastered the art of budgeting, discovering ways to optimize your expenses and make the most of your resources.

Furthermore, the mention of Japan's intricate transportation system, especially the vast train network, used to be a labyrinth that left you perplexed. Planning routes between cities or off-the-beaten-path exploration might have seemed like a daunting task. Today, you've become a maestro in navigating Japan's transportation, efficiently hopping from one destination to another.

Lastly, you might have worried about falling into tourist traps and missing out on the hidden gems that make this country so enchanting. With your newfound knowledge, you've uncovered the secrets to seeking and savoring authentic Japanese moments wherever your journey takes you.

Seeing how you've transformed these pain points into stepping stones on your path to an extraordinary Japanese adventure is incredible. This book has provided you with the tools to make your trip fulfilling and enriching. You're prepared to tackle the challenges and hiccups of Japanese travel head-on. You're ready for everything from making a solid travel plan to budgeting like a pro! Additionally, your newfound cultural wisdom ensures you'll engage with locals respectfully and avoid cultural misunderstandings. So, you won't just be a tourist but a welcomed guest in Japan.

Now, as you're about to head out on your Japanese adventure, I want to leave you with this: Don't be afraid to participate! Dive into local traditions, savor every bite of traditional dishes, explore centuries-old temples, and immerse yourself in vibrant festivals. Your journey isn't just about witnessing Japan; it's about becoming a part of it. After all, it's not just a trip; it's an amalgamation of unforgettable moments, genuine connections, and newfound appreciation for a country that's about to capture your heart.

Your Japanese journey is waiting, so make it an extraordinary one to remember. We'd love to hear about your experiences and welcome your feedback through a review wherever you purchase this book. Safe travels, and may your journey be a memorable one!

REFERENCES

About. (n.d.-a). HOSHINOYA Luxury Hotels. https://hoshinoya.com/en/about/

About. (n.d.-b). Konansou. https://www.konansou.com/eng/

About Japan's four seasons. (2016, March 22). Live Japan. https://livejapan.com/en/article-a0000283/

Acar, A. (2021, October 27). *Tea ceremony in Japan*. Tea Ceremony Japan Experiences Maikoya. https://mai-ko.com/travel/culture-in-japan/tea-ceremony/japanese-tea-ceremony/

Accommodation. (n.d.). Travel Japan. https://www.japan.travel/en/au/plan/accommodation/#:~:text=Ryokan%20(traditional%20inns)&text=Common%20elements%20to%20this%20most

Accommodation in Japan. (n.d.). Japan Experience. https://www.japan-experience.com/plan-your-trip/thematic-guides/accommodation-in-japan

Adalid, A. (2019, January 27). *Best hotels in Tokyo, Japan (per district): Budget to luxury*. I Am Aileen. https://iamaileen.com/best-hotels-in-tokyo-japan/#google_vignette

Affinati, A. (2014, September 14). *10 steps to improve your travel experience*. G+T. https://www.greenandturquoise.com/10-steps-to-improve-your-travel-experience/

Akashi Kaikyo Bridge. (n.d.). Japan Guide. https://www.japan-guide.com/e/e3559.html

Akihabara. (n.d.). Japan Guide. https://www.japan-guide.com/e/e3003.html

Akihabara area guide. (n.d.). Tokyo Cheapo. https://tokyocheapo.com/locations/central-tokyo/akihabara-central-tokyo/

Akkerman, S. (2021, July 13). *Traditional Japanese summer events: What is Tanabata?* Japan Wonder Travel Blog. https://blog.japanwondertravel.com/what-is-tanabata-26542

Albala, K. (2017, July 16). *The story of Japanese cuisine*. Wondrium Daily.

https://www.wondriumdaily.com/the-story-of-sushi-and-japanese-cuisine/

Alvarez, A. (2019, November 20). *13 best things to do in Fukuoka*. The Poor Traveler Itinerary Blog. https://www.thepoortraveler.net/2019/11/fukuoka-tourist-spots-things-to-do/

April. (2018, November 19). *A brief history of sushi and why it's so popular today*. Roka Akor. https://rokaakor.com/a-brief-history-of-sushi-and-why-its-so-popular-today/#:~:text=While%20-Japan%20is%20certainly%20the

Arima Onsen. (n.d.). Japan Guide. https://www.japan-guide.com/e/e3558.html

Aso-Kuju National Park. (n.d.). Japan Guide. https://www.japan.travel/national-parks/parks/aso-kuju/

Baker, L. (2022, December 15). *Say this before you eat: Itadakimasu!* ByFood. https://www.byfood.com/blog/culture/itadakimasu

Bales, B. (2020, January 15). *7 tips to traveling off the beaten path*. The Traveling Fool. https://thetravellingfool.com/7-tips-to-traveling-off-the-beaten-path/

Barber, C. (2014, October 7). *Ultimate comfort food: Make the best-ever homemade ramen in 3 steps*. Today. https://www.today.com/food/ultimate-comfort-food-make-homemade-ramen-3-easy-steps-2d80199816

Baseel, C. (2018, August 23). *Five reasons there's no tipping at restaurants in Japan*. SoraNews24. https://soranews24.com/2018/08/23/five-reasons-theres-no-tipping-at-restaurants-in-japan/

Basic sushi knowledge. (n.d.). Sushi University. https://sushiuniversity.jp/basicknowledge/types-of-sushi

A beginner's guide to cherry blossom viewing: How to do hanami? (2019, February). Japan Guide. https://www.japan-guide.com/e/e2011_how.html

Benton, K. (2023, January 24). *Sapporo snow festival: What to see, how to enjoy*. Unseen Japan. https://unseen-japan.com/sapporo-snow-festival-hokkaido-guide/

Best winter illuminations in Japan 2020. (2022, December 15). Japan Rail Pass. https://www.jrailpass.com/blog/winter-illuminations-japan

Borderless. (n.d.). TeamLab. https://www.teamlab.art/e/borderless-azabu

dai/

Bowing in Japan: A guide for foreigners. (2022, February 24). Interac Network. https://interacnetwork.com/bowing-in-japan/#:~:text=Bowing%20in%20Japan%20can%20be

Budget sightseeing: Tokyo subway tickets & day passes for tourists. (2020, February 7). Live Japan. https://livejapan.com/en/in-tokyo/in-pref-tokyo/in-tokyo_train_station/article-a0000207/

Budget travel - food. (n.d.). Japan Guide. https://www.japan-guide.com/e/e2028_food.html

Burkosky, E. (2017, September 14). *Common problems for tourists visiting Japan.* LinkedIn. https://www.linkedin.com/pulse/common-problems-tourists-visiting-japan-evan-burkosky/

Bus travel in Japan. (2018, September 21). Travel Japan. https://www.japan.travel/en/sg/guide/bus-travel-japan/

Buses. (n.d.). Japan Guide. https://www.japan-guide.com/planning/transportation/bus.html

Calculate your travel budget in Japan. (n.d.). Kanpai. https://www.kanpai-japan.com/japan-travel-budget-calculator

Chen, N. H. (2016, July 9). *Okonomiyaki recipe.* Just One Cookbook. https://www.justonecookbook.com/okonomiyaki/

Chopstick etiquette in Japan: Golden rules for holding & using. (2021, July 19). Link Japan Careers Inc. https://linkjapancareers.net/chopstick-etiquette-japan-using-chopsticks-in-japan/

Community reservation system. (n.d.). Kumano Travel. https://www.kumano-travel.com/en/model-itineraries/6-days-E1-kumano-kodo-trek-nakahechi#:~:text=This%20is%20the%20classic%20Kumano

Countries with the most Michelin-starred restaurants worldwide 2023. (2023, July 20). Statista. https://www.statista.com/statistics/1400971/countries-most-michelin-starred-restaurants-worldwide/#:~:text=France%20was%20the%20country%20with

Cup noodles museum. (n.d.). Japan Guide. https://www.japan-guide.com/e/e3212.html

A curious look into Japan's safety – why does your lost wallet return in Japan? (2019, November 9). Live Japan. https://livejapan.com/en/in-tokyo/in-pref-tokyo/in-akihabara/article-a0002489/

Daisetsuzan National Park. (n.d.-a). Japan Guide. https://www.japan-guide.com/e/e6775.html

Daisetsuzan National Park. (n.d.-b). Travel Japan. https://www.japan.travel/national-parks/parks/daisetsuzan/

Dayman, L. (n.d.). *Gion Kyoto: 20 must-see highlights of the geisha district*. Japan Objects. https://japanobjects.com/features/gion-kyoto

Dearsley, B., & Drillinger, M. (2023, May 11). *12 top-rated tourist attractions in Fukuoka*. PlanetWare. https://www.planetware.com/japan/fukuoka-jpn-ky-fuku.htm

Detourista, M. (2023a, February 1). *Nagano travel goals! Beautiful places to visit for first-timers*. Detourista. https://www.detourista.com/guide/nagano-attractions/

Detourista, M. (2023b, February 1). *Shirakawa-go + Gifu travel goals! Beautiful places to visit for first-timers*. Detourista. https://www.detourista.com/guide/shirakawa-go-attractions/

Diederichs, K. (2019, September 17). *Japan pocket wifi vs. Japanese SIM card*. Two Wandering Soles. https://www.twowanderingsoles.com/blog/japan-pocket-wifi-japanese-sim-card

Dining out. (2023, March 11). Japan Guide. https://www.japan-guide.com/e/e2040.html#:~:text=Paying

Discovering the delectable history of tempura. (2022, December 27). Slurrp. https://www.slurrp.com/article/discovering-the-delectable-history-of-tempura-1672154911642

Dotonbori area: The bright heart of Osaka. (n.d.). Osaka Station. https://www.osakastation.com/dotonbori-area-the-bright-heart-of-osaka/

Duncan, E. (2021, September 15). *Itadakimasu: Why using it shows good table manners*. Busuu Blog. https://blog.busuu.com/itadakimasu/

8 phrases that explore Japanese food culture. (n.d.). Google Arts & Culture. https://artsandculture.google.com/story/8-phrases-that-explore-japanese-food-culture/awXBI8Lyhfco-w?hl=en

18 travel secrets of Aomori Japan: Guide for sightseeing, shopping, and more. (2020, March 9). Live Japan. https://livejapan.com/en/in-tohoku/in-pref-aomori/in-aomori_hirosaki_hachinohe/article-a3000008/

Emergency numbers for Japan (police, fire, ambulance, etc.). (2022, October 13). Japan Mobility. https://www.japan-mobility.com/guide/emergency-numbers/japan

Emerson, R. W. (2017, November 2). *Life is a journey, not a destination*.

Caroline Gregoire Coaching. https://www.cg-four.com/if-not-a-destination-then-what

Encyclopædia Britannica. (2019). Asia - Climate. In *Encyclopædia Britannica.* https://www.britannica.com/place/Asia/Climate

Encyclopedia Britannica. (n.d.). Japanese Alps. In *Encyclopedia Britannica.* https://www.britannica.com/place/Japanese-Alps

Encyclopedia Britannica. (2019). Mount Fuji. In *Encyclopædia Britannica.* https://www.britannica.com/place/Mount-Fuji

Esa, J. (2020, October 23). *Getting around Osaka: Guide to public transportation.* TripSavvy. https://www.tripsavvy.com/osaka-public-transportation-guide-5069994

Espinas, E. (2021, August 4). *How to create a travel itinerary (A complete guide).* Passero. https://travelpassero.com/how-to-create-a-travel-itinerary/

15 best places to visit in Hakone. (2019, December 13). Hakone Japan. https://hakone-japan.com/plan-your-trip/travelog/15-best-places-to-visit-in-hakone/15-best-places-to-visit-in-hakone-en/

The 15 best things to do in Matsushima-machi. (n.d.). Tripadvisor. https://www.tripadvisor.com/Attractions-g319095-Activities-Matsushima_machi_Miyagi_gun_Miyagi_Prefecture_Tohoku.html

15 of the best places to visit in Nagano. (n.d.). Go Nagano. https://www.go-nagano.net/en/theme/id=18412

15 things to do in Shirakawa-go & where to stay. (2023, April 25). Snow Monkey Resorts. https://www.snowmonkeyresorts.com/smr/takayama-city/things-to-do-in-shirakawa-go-where-to-stay/

Flassig, S. A. (n.d.). *20 famous onsen towns in Japan & their best hot springs.* AlexRockinJapan. https://www.alexrockinjapan.com/famous-onsen-towns-in-japan-and-their-best-hot-springs/

Food & drink sector in Japan. (2020, June 26). Tokyoesque. https://tokyoesque.com/industries-japan-market/japanese-food-drink-market/

Four seasons in Japan. (2021, December 4). Japan Care Worker Guide. https://japancwg.com/8358/

Fresh food. (n.d.). Tochigi Power. https://fresh-food.tochigipower.com/en/

Fujino, K. (2023, June 28). *Japan's vending machine culture, a glimpse into the unattended payments future.* Ingenico. https://ingenico.com/apac/

newsroom/blogs/japans-vending-machine-culture-glimpse-unattended-payments-future

Fushimi Inari Shrine. (n.d.). Japan Guide. https://www.japan-guide.com/e/e3915.html

Getting around Osaka. (n.d.). Inside Osaka. https://insideosaka.com/getting-around-osaka/

Gion travel guide: Walking through Kyoto's geisha district. (2021, July 8). Japan Rail Pass. https://www.jrailpass.com/blog/gion-kyoto-travel-guide

Giving gifts in Japan. (2019, June 30). Japan Guide. https://www.japan-guide.com/e/e2004.html

Goodmacher, G. (2013, August 2). *Understanding onsen culture*. Japan Experience. https://www.japan-experience.com/plan-your-trip/to-know/understanding-japan/understanding-onsen-culture

Greenwood, V. (2016, July 27). *The comfort food that took over the world*. BBC. https://www.bbc.com/future/article/20160726-the-comfort-food-that-took-over-the-world

Guellou, O. (2019, June 26). *The popularity of theme cafés in Japan*. WorkInJapan.today. https://workinjapan.today/culture/the-popularity-of-theme-cafes-in-japan/

A guide to ramen in Japan. (n.d.). Travel Japan. https://www.japan.travel/en/guide/a-guide-to-ramen-in-japan/

A guide to Shinjuku - things to do and places to go. (2022, October 19). Gotokyo.org. https://www.gotokyo.org/en/destinations/western-tokyo/shinjuku/index.html

Hannah, D. (2019, March 13). *How to enjoy staying in a ryokan (Japanese inn)*. Japan Travel Blog. https://alljapantours.com/japan/travel/where-to-stay/Staying-in-a-Ryokan-traditional-Japanese-Inn/

Hanus , J. (2023). *Myths & legends in Kansai*. H&R Group K.K. https://morethanrelo.com/en/myths-legends-in-kansai/

Hendrieka, Anita. "Anita Hendrieka Travel Blog." Anita Hendrieka. Last modified November 8, 2023. https://www.anitahendrieka.com/facts-about-japan/

Highway buses. (n.d.). Japan Guide. https://www.japan-guide.com/e/e2366.html

Hiking in Japan. (n.d.). Travel Japan. https://www.japan.travel/en/guide/hiking/

Himeno, E. (2020, August 7). *"Thank you" in Japanese: Politeness, formality and useful phrases*. Clozemaster Blog. https://www.clozemaster.com/blog/thank-you-in-japanese/

Hiroshima Castle. (n.d.). Japan Guide. https://www.japan-guide.com/e/e3402.html

Historic Village of Hokkaido. (n.d.). Japan Guide. https://www.japan-guide.com/e/e5303.html

History of Japanese cuisine. (2020, June 4). Japan Food Style. https://japanfoodstyle.com/history-of-japanese-cuisine/

Hotel reservation. (n.d.). Toyoko Inn. https://www.toyoko-inn.com/eng/index

How and where to enjoy the four seasons in Japan. (2021). All Nippon Airways. https://www.ana.co.jp/en/in/japan-travel-planner/ideas/seasons/

How can I buy the Japan Rail Pass? How do I activate the Japan Rail Pass? (n.d.). Japan Rail Pass. https://www.jrailpass.com/faq/where-how-to-buy-japan-rail-pass#:~:text=Order%20is%20issued.-

How do you budget for travel expenses? (n.d.). SalesTrip. https://salestrip.com/faqs/how-do-you-budget-for-travel-expenses/

How to eat out in Japan: A guide to restaurants, ordering, and manners. (2019, December 17). Matcha. https://matcha-jp.com/en/8690

How to enjoy Japan's unique seasonality. (n.d.). All Nippon Airways. https://www.ana.co.jp/en/ph/japan-travel-planner/ideas/seasons/

How to hold chopsticks: The easy way how to use chopsticks properly! (2016, March 22). Live Japan. https://livejapan.com/en/article-a0000335/

How to take an onsen? | 8 rules & manners of Japanese onsen. (2019, April 23). Kashiwaya Magazine. https://www.kashiwaya.org/e/magazine/onsen/rules2.html

Hutcherson, A. (2017, November 15). *Kitchen language: What is Kaiseki?* Michelin Guide. https://guide.michelin.com/us/en/article/features/what-is-kaiseki-japanese-meal

Ian. (2015, February 26). *How to ride a bus in Japan*. Fuji-Hakone-Izu Travel Guide. http://www.fuji-travel-guide.com/news-item/taking-bus/

Imada, K. (2022, May 25). *Survey: Japan is the number one tourist destination in the world.* Time Out. https://www.timeout.com/tokyo/news/survey-japan-is-the-number-one-tourist-destination-in-the-world-052522

Important things to consider when choosing a travel destination. (2020, April 25). Mind the Travel. https://mindthetravel.com/how-to-choose-a-travel-destination-things-to-consider/

Internet access in Japan for travelers. (2019, April 26). Japan Rail Pass. https://www.jrailpass.com/blog/internet-access-japan

Internet access when visiting Japan. (2016, January 25). Accessible Japan. https://www.accessible-japan.com/internet-access-when-visiting-japan/

Introduction. (2019, May 23). The Japan Alps. https://thejapanalps.com/en/charm/

Ise. (n.d.). JapanTravel. https://en.japantravel.com/mie/ise

Ise travel guide. (n.d.). Trip.com. https://www.trip.com/travel-guide/desti nation/ise-57140/

Isuien Garden. (2019). Japan Guide. https://www.japan-guide.com/e/e4114.html

Itsukushima Shrine. (n.d.). Japan Guide. https://www.japan-guide.com/e/e3450.html

Japan. (n.d.). U.S. Embassy & Consulates in Japan. https://www.us.emb-japan.go.jp/jicc/japan-info.html#:~:text=The%20country%20is%20-divided%20into

Japan – festivals and events. (n.d.). IExplore. https://www.iexplore.com/articles/travel-guides/far-east/japan/festivals-and-events

Japan – history and culture. (n.d.). IExplore. https://www.iexplore.com/articles/travel-guides/far-east/japan/history-and-culture

Japan Alps. (n.d.). Travel Japan. https://www.japan.travel/en/destina tions/hokuriku-shinetsu/nagano/the-nagano-alps/

Japan culture shock: "Why doesn't Japan have trash cans (but Tokyo's so darn clean)?!" (2019, December 20). Live Japan. https://livejapan.com/en/in-tokyo/in-pref-tokyo/in-shibuya/article-a0002380/

Japan local railways. (n.d.). Travel Japan. https://www.japan.travel/en/plan/getting-around/other-local-railways/

Japan Rail Pass (JR Pass). (2019, October 13). Japan Guide. https://www.japan-guide.com/e/e2361.html

Japan Rail Pass price. (n.d.). Japan Rail Pass. https://www.jrailpass.com/prices#:~:text=The%20JR%20Pass%20is%20the

Japan travel cost - Average price of a vacation to Japan: Food & meal budget, daily & weekly expenses. (n.d.). Budget Your Trip. https://www.budgetyourtrip.com/japan

Japan travel tips: 9 things I wish I'd known before going to Japan. (2019, September 22). Live Japan. https://livejapan.com/en/article-a0002487/

Japan visas requirements: Do I need a visa for Japan? (2017). Japan Rail Pass. https://www.jrailpass.com/blog/japan-visa

Japan's private railway lines. (n.d.). Japan Rail Pass. https://www.jrpass.com/blog/japan-s-private-railway-lines

Japanese culture: Why should you remove your shoes? (2020, July 16). JTB Communication Design. https://me.jtbcom.co.jp/newsletters/japanese-culture-why-should-you-remove-your-shoes.html#:~:text=People%20in%20Japan%20hold%20cleanliness

Japanese history. (2019). Japan Guide. https://www.japan-guide.com/e/e641.html

The Japanese transportation system. (2018, February 27). Japaniverse. https://www.japaniverse.com/japanese-transportation-system/

Japan's missing trash cans: How does the country stay so clean? (2023, August 9). Japan Dev. https://japan-dev.com/blog/trash-cans-in-japan

Joanna Roams Free. (2023, August 16). *The ultimate guide to travelling off the beaten path.* Worldpackers. https://www.worldpackers.com/articles/travelling-off-the-beaten-path

Joyful trains. (n.d.). East Japan Railway Company. https://www.jreast.co.jp/multi/en/joyful/

JR Chuo Line in Tokyo. (n.d.). Japan Rail Pass.https://www.jrpass.com/blog/jr-chuo-line-in-tokyo

JR Yamanote Line Tokyo. (n.d.). Japan Rail Pass. https://www.jrpass.com/blog/jr-yamanote-line-tokyo

K, H. (2023, June 16). *15 best onsen towns in Japan.* Japan Web Magazine. https://jw-webmagazine.com/best-onsen-towns-in-japan/

Kabira Bay. (n.d.). Visit Ishigaki. https://visitishigaki.com/sights-activities/kabira-bay/

Kagoshima. (n.d.). Japan Guide. https://www.japan-guide.com/e/e4600.html

Kasuga Taisha. (n.d.). Japan Guide. https://www.japan-guide.com/e/e4102.html

Kiyomizudera Temple. (n.d.). Japan Guide. https://www.japan-guide.com/e/e3901.html

Kobe Harborland. (n.d.). Japan Guide. https://www.japan-guide.com/e/e3553.html

Kraft, M. (2019, August 14). *How to plan great itineraries: It all comes down to balance*. The Tour Team. https://medium.com/the-tour-team/how-to-plan-great-itineraries-it-all-comes-down-to-balance-c484dab9c088

Kumano Kodo pilgrimage trails. (n.d.). Japan Guide. https://www.japan-guide.com/e/e4952.html

Kyoto gion matsuri (gion festival). (2014). Japan Guide. https://www.japan-guide.com/e/e3942.html

Lane, G. (2022, July 18). *Best places to exchange currency in Tokyo*. Tokyo Cheapo. https://tokyocheapo.com/business/financial/show-me-the-money-cheapest-places-to-exchange-your-cash-for-yen/

Learn how to budget for a trip with travel expenses. (2022, October 19). Capital One. https://www.capitalone.com/bank/money-management/life-events/budget-your-trip/

Live Japan. (2016, March 22). *Japanese climate and population*. https://livejapan.com/en/article-a0000188/

Lynch, L. (2019, June 26). *Easy okonomiyaki recipe (savory Japanese pancakes)*. A Food Lover's Kitchen. https://afoodloverskitchen.com/easy-okonomiyaki-recipe-savory-japanese-pancakes/

Lytwyn, L. (2021, February 19). *Everything you need to know about ryokans in Japan, a guide to your first stay*. The Creative Adventurer. https://thecreativeadventurer.com/everything-you-need-to-know-about-ryokans-in-japan-a-guide-to-your-first-stay/

M, A. (2021, October 3). *Calling a cab, Japan style*. Japan Mobility. https://www.japan-mobility.com/guide/taxis-in-japan

Mae-Gene. (2017, September 29). *8 things to do on Naoshima Island,*

Japan's art island. The Wandering Suitcase. https://www.thewanderingsuitcase.com/naoshima-island/

Mansfield, S. (2023, May 16). *Japan's vending machine culture is ahead of the curve*. Nikkei Asia. https://asia.nikkei.com/Editor-s-Picks/Tea-Leaves/Japan-s-vending-machine-culture-is-ahead-of-the-curve

Matcha: The heart of the Japanese tea ceremony. (2009, August 24). English Tea Store. https://blog.englishteastore.com/2009/08/24/matcha-the-heart-of-the-japenese-tea-ceremony/

Matsushima. (n.d.). Japan Guide. https://www.japan-guide.com/e/e5100.html

Max, A. (2020, February 23). *6 places to find affordable Kobe beef in Kobe, Japan*. Dame Cacao. https://damecacao.com/affordable-kobe-beef-in-kobe-japan/

Mayu. (2020, March 5). *Food expenses for travel in Japan - 1,000 yen meals and budget tips*. Matcha. https://matcha-jp.com/en/2532

Meiji Shrine. (n.d.). Japan Guide. https://www.japan-guide.com/e/e3002.html#:~:text=Meiji%20Shrine%20

Milner, R. (2023, March 20). *Japan on a budget: 17 ways to get more for your yen*. Lonely Planet. https://www.lonelyplanet.com/articles/japan-on-a-budget

Miseviciute, A. (2019, July 28). *The art of tempura making by Japan's best master Shuji Niitome*. Pen Magazine International. https://pen-online.com/food/the-art-of-tempura-making-by-japans-best-master-shuji-niitome/

Miyajima. (n.d.). Japan Guide. https://www.japan-guide.com/e/e3401.html

Miyajima guide: Things to do and where to visit. (2023, October 4). Japan Cheapo. https://japancheapo.com/entertainment/miyajima-sightseeing-guide/

Monzon, R. (2022, December 27). *Japan train travel made easy: How to activate the JR Pass and use exchange orders*. Klook Travel. https://www.klook.com/en-AU/blog/jr-pass-redemption-guide/

Mount Fuji. (2019). Japan Guide. https://www.japan-guide.com/e/e2172.html

Mount Wakakusayama. (n.d.). Japan Guide. https://www.japan-guide.com/e/e4113.html

Mt. fuji: More than a mountain. (n.d.). Travel Japan. https://www.japan.travel/en/fuji-guide/mt-fuji-more-than-a-mountain/

Must-see night view in Sapporo! (2016, July 26). Hokkaido Labo. https://hokkaido-labo.com/en/moiwa-mountain-night-view-585

Nagoya Castle. (2018). Nagoya Castle Official Website. https://www.nagoyajo.city.nagoya.jp/en/

Naho_B_M. (2018, February 20). *12 best themed cafes and restaurants to visit in Tokyo 2020.* Japan Web Magazine. https://jw-webmagazine.com/10-best-themed-cafes-and-restaurants-to-visit-in-tokyo-2018-74b9b7261099/

Naho_B_M. (2019, April 8). *10 best beaches on Okinawa main island.* Japan Web Magazine. https://jw-webmagazine.com/10-best-beaches-on-okinawa-main-island-7bfe1fd5b84e/

Nakaya, Rion. "Sampuru: How is Japanese Fake Food Made?" The Kid Should See This. Last modified September 18, 2023. https://thekid shouldseethis.com/post/sampuru-how-is-japanese-fake-food-made

Naoshima travel guide. (n.d.). Trip.com. https://www.trip.com/travel-guide/destination/naoshima-60691/

Nara Park. (n.d.). Japan Guide. https://www.japan-guide.com/e/e4103.html

Nast, C. (2021, September 26). *How tempura evolved from a Portuguese staple to a Japanese art.* Epicurious. https://www.epicurious.com/expert-advice/how-tempura-evolved-from-a-portuguese-staple-to-a-japanese-art-article

Natasha. (2020, January 5). *Guide to the best pocket WIFI and SIM cards for traveling in Japan.* Away from Origin. https://awayfromorigin.com/travel/asia/japan/wifi-sim-japan/

Nikko. (n.d.). Japan Guide. https://www.japan-guide.com/e/e3800.html

The 9 best character cafes you must visit in Japan. (2023, September). ZenMarket. https://zenmarket.jp/en/blog/post/8026/character-cafes-japan

9 Hours Capsule Hotel. (n.d.). https://ninehours.co.jp/

9 Hours Suidobashi. (n.d.). Booking.com. https://shorturl.at/jzAY0

Nui. Hostel & Bar Lounge. (n.d.). Booking.com. https://shorturl.at/hnAO6

Obon. (2019, January 13). Japan Guide. https://www.japan-guide.com/e/e2286.html

Obon festival guide: Meaning, traditions and dates. (2022, December 15). Japan Rail Pass. https://www.jrailpass.com/blog/obon-festival-in-japan

Ogasawara Islands. (n.d.-a). Japan Guide. https://www.japan-guide.com/e/e8200.html

Ogasawara Islands. (n.d.-b). UNESCO World Heritage Centre. https://whc.unesco.org/en/list/1362/

Okinawa Churaumi Aquarium. (2010). Travel Japan. https://www.japan.travel/en/spot/581/

Okonomiyaki. (n.d.). Japan Guide. https://www.japan-guide.com/r/e100.html

Okonomiyaki - Japanese savoury pancakes. (2020, October 14). Wandercooks. https://www.wandercooks.com/okonomiyaki-japanese-savoury-pancakes/

Okonomiyaki history. (n.d.). Okonomiyaki World. https://okonomiyakiworld.com/Okonomiyaki-History.html#:~:text=Okonomiyaki%20was%20invented%20in%20Japan

Oliver, R. (2014, September 29). *Japanese gifting etiquette: Learn about the gift giving ritual.* Truly Experiences Blog. https://trulyexperiences.com/blog/japanese-gifting-etiquette/

Osaka Castle. (n.d.). Japan Guide. https://www.japan-guide.com/e/e4000.html

Osu Kannon Temple. (n.d.). Japan Guide. https://www.japan-guide.com/e/e3306.html

Osu Shopping District. (n.d.). Visit Nagoya. https://www.nagoya-info.jp/en/spot/detail/19/

Peace Memorial Park. (n.d.). Japan Guide. https://www.japan-guide.com/e/e3400.html

Peñascal, M. (2022, June 6). *Accommodations in Japan: A comprehensive guide.* VOYAPON. https://voyapon.com/accommodations-in-japan/

Philosopher's path. (n.d.). Japan Guide. https://www.japan-guide.com/e/e3906.html

Polite Japanese language. (2011, December 9). Japan Reference. https://jref.com/articles/polite-japanese-language.64/

Politeness and formality in Japanese. (2015). Japanese Professor. https://

www.japaneseprofessor.com/lessons/beginning/politeness-and-formality/

Politeness in Japanese. (2017, March 15). GaijinPot Study. https://study.gaijinpot.com/lesson/online-lessons/politeness-in-japanese/#:~:text=Polite%20speech%20in%20Japanese%20is

Prepaid IC cards in Japan: How to use. (2023, August 14). Japan Rail Pass. https://www.jrailpass.com/blog/using-japanese-ic-cards

Prices and living costs in Japan. (2018, November 18). Japan Guide. https://www.japan-guide.com/e/e2202.html

Prices/Sales locations. (n.d.). Greater Tokyo Pass. https://greater-tokyo-pass.jp/en/ticket/

Private lines in Japan. (2916, December 28). Japan Rail Pass. https://www.japan-rail-pass.com/plan-your-trip/travel-by-train/train-in-japan/private-lines-in-japan

Procedures for making reservations online. (2023). All Nippon Airways. https://www.ana.co.jp/en/ph/plan-book/promotions/special-fares/

Promote your products / services in Japan (organic food / green / digital). (n.d.). EU-Japan Centre. https://www.eu-japan.eu/promote-your-products-services-japan-organic-food-green-digital

Quantum leap in transportation. (n.d.). SCMAGLEV. https://scmaglev.jr-central-global.com/

Quintana, K. (2022, August 17). *The culture behind Japanese onsen.* Bokksu. https://www.bokksu.com/blogs/news/japanese-onsen

Rabbit Island (Okunoshima). (n.d.). Travel Japan. https://www.japan.travel/en/spot/871/

Ramen Alley. (2020, June 12). Hokkaido Guide. https://hokkaidoguide.com/ramen-alley/

Ramen: One of the world's favorite comfort food. (2012, November 24). Day Translations. https://www.daytranslations.com/blog/ramen-worlds-favorite-food/

Regional sushi specialties. (n.d.). Sushiya Sansaro. https://www.sushiya.de/en/sushi/sushi-sorten/regionale-sushi-spezialitaeten/

Renting a pocket wi-fi router & SIM card in Japan: Options, advice & where to book. (2023, July 13). Live Japan. https://livejapan.com/en/article-a0002406/

Reserving seats & boarding the Bullet Train. (n.d.). JRPass. https://www.jrpass.com/blog/reserving-seats-boarding-the-bullet-train

Robertshaw, E. (2016, January 26). *8 rules for Japanese chopstick etiquette.* Andiamo. https://www.andiamo.co.uk/blog/8-rules-for-japanese-chopstick-etiquette/

Rodgers, G. (2019). *Know how and when to bow in Japan before you go.* TripSavvy. https://www.tripsavvy.com/when-to-bow-in-japan-1458314

The role of matcha tea in traditional Japanese tea ceremony. (2023, April 27). Matcha Outlet. https://matchaoutlet.com/blogs/articles/the-role-of-matcha-tea-in-traditional-japanese-tea-ceremony

Rowan, C. (2023, February 10). *Japan's unique vending machine culture!* Arigato Travel. https://arigatojapan.co.jp/japans-unique-vending-machine-culture/

Rowthorn, C. (2013). *Arashiyama Bamboo Grove.* Inside Kyoto. https://www.insidekyoto.com/arashiyama-bamboo-grove

Ryukyu Mura. (n.d.). Japan Guide. https://www.japan-guide.com/e/e7121.html

Sabia, S. (2020, November 13). *25 best things to do in Kumamoto, one of Japan's most picturesque regions.* Tsunagu Japan. https://www.tsunagu japan.com/7-popular-picturesque-spots-kumamoto/

Sankeien Garden. (n.d.). Japan Guide. https://www.japan-guide.com/e/e3205.html

The Sapporo Snow Festival. (2013, July 1). Travel Japan. https://www.japan.travel/en/us/blog/the-sapporo-snow-festival/

Senda, M. (2020, July 10). *The 6 best discount travel & rail passes to Japan on a budget.* VOYAPON. https://voyapon.com/special-tourist-discount-passes-guide-for-japan/#:~:text=Greater%20Tokyo%20Pass

Shephard, J. (2018, December 2). *How to discover off the beaten path destinations.* The Lost Passport. https://www.thelostpassport.com/off-the-beaten-path/

Shibayama, K. (2022, February 24). *Levels of formality in Japanese (how to know when to use which).* Argos Multilingual. https://www.argosmulti lingual.com/blog/levels-of-formality-in-japanese-how-to-know-when-to-use-which

Shimizu, M. (2021, June 29). *A complete guide to ryokan: How to enjoy tradi-*

tional stay in Japan. Japan Wonder Travel Blog. https://blog.japanwondertravel.com/complete-guide-to-ryokan-26906

Shin-Kobe Ropeway. (n.d.). Japan Guide. https://www.japan-guide.com/e/e3563.html

Shinjuku. (n.d.). Japan Guide. https://www.japan-guide.com/e/e3011.html

The Shinkansen bullet train in Japan. (n.d.). Asia Highlights. https://www.asiahighlights.com/japan/shinkansen-bullet-train

Shinkansen (Japanese bullet train). (n.d.). Japan Guide. https://www.japan-guide.com/e/e2018.html

Shiretoko. (n.d.). UNESCO World Heritage Centre. https://whc.unesco.org/en/list/1193/#:~:text=Shiretoko%20is%20one%20of%20the

Shiretoko travel guide. (2019, March). Japan Guide. https://www.japan-guide.com/e/e6850.html

Shopping at a supermarket. (2021, January 12). Japan Experience. https://www.japan-experience.com/plan-your-trip/to-know/traveling-japan/shopping-at-a-supermarket

Shukkeien Garden. (n.d.). Japan Guide. https://www.japan-guide.com/e/e3403.html

Shuri Castle. (n.d.). Japan Guide. https://www.japan-guide.com/e/e7103.html

6 reasons why you should visit Japan at least once in your life. (2020, September 3). Japan Wonder Travel Blog. https://blog.japanwondertravel.com/reason-to-visit-japan-14343

16 fun things to do in Kagoshima - places to go, local food & sightseeing tips. (n.d.). Live Japan. https://livejapan.com/en/in-tokyo/in-pref-other/in-pref-kagoshima/article-a0004956/

Spacey, J. (2009, September 2). *35 problems you will have in Japan.* Japan Talk. https://www.japan-talk.com/jt/new/japan-travel-challenges

Stefon, M. (2019). Bon festival. In *Encyclopædia Britannica.* https://www.britannica.com/story/bon-festival

Subway in Japan. (n.d.). Travel Japan. https://www.japan.travel/en/plan/getting-around/subways/

Sumiyoshi Taisha. (n.d.). Japan Guide. https://www.japan-guide.com/e/e4007.html

Sunelle. (2018, April 8). *Factors to consider when choosing a travel destination*. Focused Travels. https://focusedtravels.com/travel-destination

Suzuki, M. (2016, September 20). *The meaning of itadakimasu*. Tofugu. https://www.tofugu.com/japanese/itadakimasu-meaning/#:~:text=The%20Meaning%20of%20Itadakimasu

Sylvia. (2022, November 9). *Best 15 Japan travel apps to keep your trip stress-free*. Wapiti Travel. https://www.wapititravel.com/blog/en/japan-travel-apps/

Takayama. (n.d.). Japan Guide. https://www.japan-guide.com/e/e5900.html

Tan, B. (2023, July 27). *Trains in Japan: First-timer's guide to Japan's rail network*. Klook. https://www.klook.com/en-US/blog/trains-in-japan-guide/

Tanabata. (2019, January 13). Japan Guide. https://www.japan-guide.com/e/e2283.html

Tanabata – story of two star-crossed lovers. (2014, July 6). Japan Suite. https://www.japan-suite.com/blog/2014/7/6/tanabata-story-of-two-star-crossed-lovers

Taxi. (n.d.). Japan Guide. https://www.japan-guide.com/e/e2021.html

Taxis in Japan: Etiquette & how much they cost. (2022, March 28). Interac Network. https://interacnetwork.com/taxis-in-japan/

Tea in Japan. (n.d.). Japan Guide. https://www.japan-guide.com/e/e2041.html

The teaware you need to host a Japanese matcha green tea ceremony. (n.d.). Teaologists. https://teaologists.co.uk/blogs/teaologists-health-habit-blog/which-tools-and-what-teaware-you-need-for-hosting-a-japanese-matcha-gree-tea-ceremony-at-home

Tempura. (n.d.). Japan Guide. https://www.japan-guide.com/r/e106.html

Tenjinbashisuji shopping street. (n.d.). Osaka Info. https://osaka-info.jp/en/spot/tenjimbashisuji-shopping-street/

10 best apps for traveling in Japan. (2022, October 14). Japan Rail Pass. https://www.jrailpass.com/blog/best-apps-travel-japan

10 best onsen and onsen towns in Japan. (2018, October 1). Japan Rail Pass. https://www.jrailpass.com/blog/best-onsen-in-japan

10 best places to visit in Kanazawa. (2020, October 8). Japan Wonder

Travel. https://blog.japanwondertravel.com/best-places-to-visit-in-kanazawa-20237

The 10 best tourist spots in kurashiki 2023: Things to do & places to go. (n.d.). Tripadvisor. https://www.tripadvisor.com.ph/Attractions-g298133-Activities-Kurashiki_Okayama_Prefecture_Chugoku.html

10 tips for flawless itinerary planning. (2015, May 29). Leisure Group Travel. https://leisuregrouptravel.com/10-tips-for-flawless-itinerary-planning/

10 tips for how to get cheap tickets 2023. (2023, September 14). Trip.com. https://www.trip.com/hot/articles/how-to-get-cheap-flight-tickets.html

There is no tipping culture in Japan. (2020, June 22). FromJapan. https://fromjapan.info/travel-tips-about-no-tipping-culture-in-japan/

Theri. (2018, May 25). *Why you should visit a theme café in Japan! Featuring Cinnamoroll & Sumikko Gurashi!* Komonogatari. https://www.komonogatari.com/2018/05/25/why-you-should-visit-a-theme-cafe-in-japan-cinamoroll-sumikko-gurashi/

Todaiji Temple. (n.d.). Japan Guide. https://www.japan-guide.com/e/e4100.html

Tokyo Disneyland. (2019). Japan Guide. https://www.japan-guide.com/e/e3016_land.html

Tokyo Inn. (n.d.). Booking.com. https://shorturl.at/juyNV

The Tokyo subway system explained with map. (n.d.). Go Tokyo. https://www.gotokyo.org/en/plan/getting-around/subways/index.html#:~:text=The%20largest%20operator%20of%20subway

Took, N. (2017, September 5). *8 reasons why budget travel is the best way to do it*. Contiki. https://www.contiki.com/six-two/article/8-reasons-budget-travel/

Top etiquette tips when visiting temples and shrines in Japan. (n.d.). Japan Airlines. https://www.jal.co.jp/ru/en/guide-to-japan/plan-your-trip/tips/what-to-know-temple-and-shrine-visit-in-japan.html#:

"TOP 17 JAPANESE CULTURE QUOTES." A-Z Quotes. Accessed November 22, 2023. https://www.azquotes.com/quotes/topics/japanese-culture.html.

Toyota-related attractions. (n.d.). Japan Guide. https://www.japan-guide.com/e/e3308.html

Train travel in Japan: A complete guide. (2023, July 31). Japan Rail Pass. https://www.jrailpass.com/blog/japanese-trains

Trains. (n.d.). Japan Guide. https://www.japan-guide.com/e/e2019.html

Transportation in Japan. (n.d.). Travel Japan. https://www.japan.travel/en/plan/getting-around/

Transportation in Japan: Buses. (n.d.). DiGJAPAN! https://digjapan.travel/en/basic/detail/id=9561

Travel goals: Inspiring ideas and how to achieve them. (2023, July 31). Worldpackers. https://www.worldpackers.com/articles/travel-goals

Traveling off the beaten path - how to uncover hidden gems. (2023, March 3). ForSomethingMore. https://forsomethingmore.com/traveling-off-the-beaten-path-hidden-gems/

20 best things to do in Shinjuku. (2017, April 27). Japan Web Magazine. https://jw-webmagazine.com/things-to-do-in-shin juku/#:~:text=Shinjuku%20is%20well%2Dknown%20for

20 fun things to do in Nikko: Recommendations for first-time visitors | LIVE JAPAN travel guide. (2020, October 21). Live Japan. https://livejapan.com/en/in-tokyo/in-pref-tochigi/in-nikko/article-a0005173/

25 things to do around Kanazawa & where to stay. (n.d.). Snow Monkey Resorts. https://www.snowmonkeyresorts.com/smr/kanazawa/things-to-do-in-around-kanazawa/

25 things to do around Takayama & where to stay. (2023, July 25). Snow Monkey Resorts. https://www.snowmonkeyresorts.com/smr/takayama-city/things-to-do-in-around-takayama/

23 places to visit in Aomori - seafood, outdoors, and more. (2023, July 23). Matcha. https://matcha-jp.com/en/7562

Types of sushi. (n.d.). WebstaurantStore. https://www.webstaurantstore.com/blog/3906/types-of-sushi.html

Types of trains in Japan. (n.d.). Japan Rail Pass. https://www.jrpass.com/trains-in-japan#:~:text=JR%20Group%20is%20made%20up

Uehara, K. (2022, September 12). *Nozawana - the village pickle.* Nozawa Hospitality. https://www.nozawahospitality.com/post/nozawana-the-village-pickle

Ultimate guide to ordering food in Japanese. (2022, February 23). Japan Switch. https://japanswitch.com/ultimate-guide-to-ordering-food-in-japanese/

Ultimate guide to seasons in Japan. (2021, June 3). Japan Switch. https://japanswitch.com/ultimate-guide-to-seasons-in-japan/#:~:text=In%20Japan%2C%20they%20have%20the

Universal Studios Japan. (n.d.). Tripadvisor. https://www.tripadvisor.com/Attraction_Review-g298566-d320976-Reviews-Universal_Studios_Japan-Osaka_Osaka_Prefecture_Kinki.html

Uppink, L., & Soshkin, M. (2022, May 24). *Travel & tourism development index 2021: Rebuilding for a sustainable and resilient future.* World Economic Forum. https://www.weforum.org/reports/travel-and-tourism-development-index-2021

Useful tickets in Tokyo. (n.d.). Travel Japan. https://www.japan.travel/en/au/plan/useful-tickets-tokyo/

Vinluan, K. (2018, June 18). *Hacks for dealing with dietary needs in Japan.* All about Japan. https://allabout-japan.com/en/article/5988/

Weldon, S. (2019, August 10). *What you need to know about dietary restrictions in Japan.* Japan and More. https://japanandmore.com/dietary-restrictions-in-japan/

What is Hanami: The fun way Japanese enjoy sakura viewing! (2019, March 31). Live Japan. https://livejapan.com/en/article-a0000708/

What is included in the Japan Rail Pass? (n.d.). Japan Rail Pass. https://www.jrailpass.com/faq/japan-rail-pass-trains-included

What is JR? Learn about Japan Railway train networks and difference from Non JR train. (2011, April 2). JPRail. https://jprail.com/travel-informations/learn-more-about-japan-railways-trains-and-networks.html

What is kaiseki? Complete guide to beautiful art of Japanese cuisine. (2021, September 8). Japan Wonder Travel Blog. https://blog.japanwondertravel.com/what-is-kaiseki-cuisine-24663

What is the Matsuri (Japanese cultural festival)? (n.d.). All Nippon Airways. https://www.ana.co.jp/en/jp/japan-travel-planner/japanese-festival-omatsuri/0000001.html#:~:text=The%20original%20purpose%20of%20the

Why it's important to budget for travel. (2019, April 9). ShareSource. https://www.sharesource.com.au/blogs/the-big-picture/why-its-important-to-budget-for-travel

Why travel to Japan? 20 best reasons to visit it. (2020, April 17). Japan Rail Pass. https://www.jrailpass.com/blog/why-travel-to-japan

Winter illuminations. (n.d.). Japan Guide. https://www.japan-guide.com/e/e2304.html

Yagisawa, E. (2019a, June 5). *Etiquette at shrines and temples: A step-by-step guide*. JapanTravel. https://en.japantravel.com/guide/shrine-temple-etiquette/20924

Yagisawa, E. (2019b, July 21). *Emergency contact information when in Japan*. JapanTravel. https://en.japantravel.com/guide/contact-info-during-emergencies/21736

Yanaka. (n.d.). Japan Guide. https://www.japan-guide.com/e/e3068.html

Yokohama Chinatown. (n.d.). Japan Guide. https://www.japan-guide.com/e/e3201.html

Yokohama Landmark Tower. (n.d.). Live Japan. https://livejapan.com/en/in-tokyo/in-pref-kanagawa/in-minatomirai21_chinatown/spot-lj0000595/

Yokohama travel: Minato Mirai 21. (n.d.). Japan Guide. https://www.japan-guide.com/e/e3200.html

Yong, K. L. (2018, September 10). *7 Japanese folklore stories to know for your Japanese holiday*. WanderWisdom. https://wanderwisdom.com/travel-destinations/7-Japanese-Folklore-Stories

Yong, N. (2023, July 1). *Hachiko: The world's most loyal dog turns 100. BBC News*. https://www.bbc.com/news/world-asia-65259426

Yu, E., & Sealy, A. (2016, August 26). *A beginner's guide to kaiseki, the world's finest meal*. CNN. https://edition.cnn.com/travel/article/guide-to-kaiseki-cuisine/index.html

Zuleta, A. (2014, July 15). *A guide to tipping in Japan*. Boutique Japan. https://boutiquejapan.com/tipping-in-japan/#:~:text=Tipping%20in%20Japan%20is%20not

Zuleta, A. (2019, February 16). *When is the best time to visit Japan?* Boutique Japan. https://boutiquejapan.com/when-is-the-best-time-of-year-to-visit-japan/

Zuleta, A. (2022, December 20). *Traveling to Japan with food allergies and dietary restrictions*. Boutique Japan. https://boutiquejapan.com/dietary-requirements-japan/

Made in the USA
Las Vegas, NV
19 August 2024